THE POWER OF THE
PROPHETIC
BLESSING

JOHN HAGEE
NEW YORK TIMES BEST-SELLING AUTHOR

WORTHY
PUBLISHING

© 2012 by John Hagee

Published by Worthy Publishing, a division of Worthy Media, Inc., 134 Franklin Road, Suite 200, Brentwood, Tennessee 37027.

HELPING PEOPLE EXPERIENCE THE HEART OF GOD

eBook available at www.worthypublishing.com

Audio distributed through Oasis Audio; visit www.oasisaudio.com

Library of Congress Control Number: 2012941812

For foreign and subsidiary rights, contact Riggins International Rights Services, Inc.; www.rigginsrights.com

ISBN: 978-1-61795-077-3 (hardcover w/jacket)

Cover Design: LUCAS Art & Design, Jenison, MI
Cover Photography: Masterfile Images
Interior Design and Typesetting: Kimberly Sagmiller, Fudge Creative

Printed in the United States of America
12 13 14 15 16 17 LBM 8 7 6 5 4 3 2 1

LOVINGLY DEDICATED

to

the most wonderful grandchildren on planet earth

Mckenzie Rene, Kassidee Nicole, Micah Elizabeth, Hannah Rose,
Victoria Grace, Olivia Jordan, Elliana Rae, Caroline Elizabeth,
John William, William Christopher, Joel Charles, and Wyatt Scott.
The Lord bless you and keep you; the Lord make His
face shine upon you, and be gracious to you: the Lord lift
up His countenance upon you and give you peace.
May the blessings and favor of the Lord rest upon your heart,
soul, mind, and body all the days of your life.
Love, Papa

CONTENTS

Section 1:

DEFINING THE PROPHETIC AND PRIESTLY BLESSINGS

CHAPTER ONE

THE POWER OF THE PROPHETIC BLESSING

Let peoples serve you,
And nations bow down to you.
Be master over your brethren,
And let your mother's sons bow down to you.
Cursed be everyone who curses you,
And blessed be those who bless you!

—GENESIS 27:29

Mankind has forever been searching for the mystery ingredient that will guarantee the good life!

Ponce de León searched for the proverbial fountain of youth. He didn't find it!

Crusaders in the Middle Ages killed and conquered multiplied thousands in the mindless pursuit of the Golden

Chalice that would guarantee eternal life. They never found it!

Citizens of the twenty-first century are spending time and treasure crisscrossing the planet in luxurious jets, opulent ocean liners, and every motorized vehicle known to man trying to find a mystical Shangri-La that will bring them to the good life. It has not been discovered!

That supernatural something is not a mystical place; it's not a rare artifact you hold in your hand; it's not a magical substance you drink; it's not an enchanted kiss that transforms the ugly frog into Prince Charming.

The only supernatural ingredient that produces the good life became a reality thousands of years before Jesus of Nazareth was born in Bethlehem's manger. It was before Solomon dedicated the second temple and the glory of God enveloped that house of worship until none could stand.

It was a reality before David killed Goliath and became the king of Israel, birthing the Golden Age for the chosen people. *That supernatural something* was introduced in the book of Genesis by God Almighty as He spoke and released the power of the Prophetic Blessing over the lives of Adam and Eve.

The Prophetic Blessing is a spoken declaration by a spiritual authority over the life of an individual. The words of the blessing carry the power to control and direct the life of the person over whom they have been spoken. The Prophetic Blessing will revolutionize your life, and the lives of your children and grandchildren, to rise to a higher level of accomplishment, creating spiritual, physical, emotional, and relational prosperity.

The power and permanence of the Prophetic Blessing have been clearly charted over the centuries in sacred Scripture. The Jewish people have obeyed the principles and received the benefits of the blessing; however, its potential has been sadly overlooked by most Christians for over two thousand years. This transforming supernatural blessing spoken by spiritual authority has the power to sculpt your life for today, tomorrow, and forever!

BRIEF BIBLE HISTORY OF THE BLESSINGS

When God created Adam and Eve in the Garden of Eden, the first thing He did for this initial marriage in recorded history was to bless it. Genesis 1:28 records these words:

> *Then God blessed them, and God said to them, "Be fruitful and multiply; fill the earth and subdue it; have dominion over the fish of the sea, over the birds of the air, and over every living thing that moves on the earth."*

It is significant to remember that the first miracle Jesus performed was at a wedding. By its creation and by the miracle of transforming water to wine, God the Father and Jesus the Son bestowed their blessings upon the union of marriage. The world has certainly forgotten the sacredness of the holy matrimony of a man and a woman as well as the blessing of bearing children within that covenant relationship.

The next blessing given in Scripture was God's blessing of Abraham, found in Genesis 12:1–3, creating the nation of Israel and what became known as the Jewish people:

> *Now the LORD had said to Abram:*
> *"Get out of your country,*
> *From your family*
> *And from your father's house,*
> *To a land [Israel] that I will show you.*
> *I will make you a great nation;*
> *I will bless you*
> *And make your name great;*
> *And you shall be a blessing.*
> *I will bless those who bless you [Israel and the Jewish people],*
> *And I will curse him who curses you;*
> *And in you all the families of the earth shall be blessed."*

This blessing—assuring the creation and establishment of the state of Israel—is the theological cornerstone of the greatest controversy in the Middle East, from the time of Abraham to the twenty-first century. However, the fact remains that God—the Maker of heaven and earth—created the nation of Israel through His divinely Spoken Word and therefore the blessing can never be revoked or annulled. "I will make you a great nation; I will bless you and make your name great" (v. 2).

The parade of blessing continues as Isaac blessed Jacob, and not Esau. As the firstborn, Esau was due to receive the better blessing, but Jacob and his mother, Rebekah, deceived Isaac into giving the blessing to Jacob. When Esau discovered that the blessing of the firstborn had been given to his younger brother, he knelt before his aged father and passionately begged, "Bless me—me also, O my father!" (Genesis 27:34).

The words of Esau have been echoed across the centuries by other sons who have missed out on the greatest earthly gift their father could give them—his blessing. This deep emotional pain has created family divisions lasting a lifetime and, in some cases, for centuries.

Scripture records that it was Esau's descendants, the Amalekites (Genesis 36:12), who attacked the children of Israel when they crossed the Red Sea bound for freedom and their new home in the Promised Land (Exodus 17:8–16). Haman, the Hitler of the Old Testament who plotted to exterminate the Jews of the Persian Empire, was a descendant of Esau (Esther 3:10).

Esau craved his father's blessing until the day he died, passing on the evil seed of murder and revenge that would leave the world covered with blood—because of the blessing his father denied him.

The blessing continued in the New Testament with a Jewish rabbi, Jesus of Nazareth, as He sat on a rock by the Sea of Galilee. Christ revealed to the multitudes the foundational principles of our faith through what has become known as the Sermon on the Mount, which includes eight Prophetic Blessings known as the Beatitudes.

In Scripture, the number eight represents new beginnings. Circumcision on the eighth day is a supernatural prophecy of the renewal that comes through entrance into God's covenant for the land of Israel. When God closed the door on the ark, there were eight people aboard; they were the new beginning of mankind. The eight Prophetic Blessings of Jesus in the Beatitudes represent a new beginning in what would in time be called Christianity.

These eight Prophetic Blessings spoken from the mouth of the Son of God—our ultimate spiritual authority—are meant for every person on earth. They have the power to resurrect your dead marriage, bring you supernatural joy, provide you peace of mind, create a healthy self-esteem, and help establish the unshakable foundations to endure life's greatest storms.

From time to time, Jesus paused from teaching the multitudes to bless the children. The Gospel of St. Mark records: "He took them up in His arms, laid His hands on them, and blessed them" (10:16).

What did He say? He said what rabbis and Jewish fathers have been saying for thousands of years: "The LORD make His face shine upon you, and be gracious to you; the LORD lift up His countenance upon you, and give you peace" (Numbers 6:25–26). And then Jesus—and Jewish fathers—as spiritual authority, spoke into existence the future their spiritual eyes could see for the children. This is the power of the Prophetic Blessing. If Jesus took time to bless the children, why don't we?

The last picture we have of Jesus in Scripture is on the Mount of Transfiguration saying farewell to His disciples. As He rose into the heavens, He looked down on His devoted followers and blessed them. The Gospel of St. Luke records: "And He led them out as far as Bethany, and He lifted up His hands and blessed them. Now it came to pass, while He blessed them, that He was parted from them and carried up into heaven" (24:50–51).

ISAAC'S STORY

Let's revisit the story of Isaac and his two sons, Esau and Jacob, found in Genesis 27, to further illustrate this profound principle of the spoken blessing. A confused and weak-eyed Isaac was tricked into declaring the Prophetic Blessing over his younger son:

> *Let peoples serve you,*
> *And nations bow down to you.*
> *Be master over your brethren,*
> *And let your mother's sons bow down to you.*
> *Cursed be everyone who curses you,*
> *And blessed be those who bless you! (v. 29)*

Later, after Jacob and his mother's deceitfulness had been realized by all, Esau begged for his father's blessing, but it did not come; Isaac had already proclaimed the blessing over Jacob. The spoken blessing could not be revoked, transferred, or surpassed.

Instead, Isaac spoke what seemed more like a curse than a blessing over his eldest son, Esau.

> *By your sword you shall live,*
> *And you shall serve your brother;*
> *And it shall come to pass, when you become restless,*
> *That you shall break his yoke from your neck. (v. 40)*

The father's supernatural impartations over his sons came to pass just as they were spoken.

Isaac's blessing over Jacob, which included the inheritance of the land, had three components. The first was the promise of prosperity: Israel now has more high-tech start-ups and a larger venture capital industry per capita than any other country in the world.[1]

The second component was the promise of dominion. Ever since God established the title deed for Israel in the land covenant of Genesis 15, the Jewish people have maintained a presence in Israel; and with the rebirth of the state of Israel in 1948, the sons of Jacob (Israel) ruled once again over the sons of Esau. Because of the covenant given by God, who owned the land as Creator, the Jewish people do not occupy the land . . . they own it!

The third and final component of Isaac's proclamation

over Jacob was the distinction between the blessings and the curses first set forth by God in Genesis 12; history has recorded God's judgments over the nations that have cursed the Jewish people.

No power on earth, no presidential election or United Nations resolution, can ever change the power of the Prophetic Blessing!

The Jewish people have excelled throughout history in the fields of medicine, technology, literature, science, the arts, and much more. There is no rational explanation other than this success is a direct result of the supernatural power of the Prophetic Blessing!

There are an estimated 14.3 million Jewish people within a worldwide population of 6.23 billion, making them .0021 percent of the total populace. Yet since 1947, in that minuscule percentage of the world's inhabitants, the Jewish people have been awarded the largest percentage (27 percent) of Nobel Prizes, even after the Holocaust destroyed one-third of their numbers.[2]

The logical answer for the historical accomplishment and prosperity of the Jewish people is the power of the Prophetic Blessing that fathers and mothers have spoken over their beloved children every Sabbath throughout the generations. The Jewish people have not only *released* the blessing; they have also *received* the blessing and carried it into their lives, accomplishing every word spoken over them.

Some will question the theological concept that the power of the spoken blessing is prophetic. Let's allow the guiding light of the Word of God to reveal the answer.

Isaac blessed Jacob and Esau, and both blessings came true exactly as spoken. Jacob blessed his twelve sons and two grandsons, Manasseh and Ephraim. Those blessings came true exactly as spoken. Jesus blessed His twelve disciples, saying, "You are the salt of the earth" and "the light of the world" (Matthew 5:13–14).

At the time Jesus spoke this Prophetic Blessing over His disciples, they were saturated with serious character flaws. If Jesus had hired a Jerusalem management firm to give Him an evaluation of the emotional profiles of His twelve disciples at the time He proclaimed the blessing over their lives, it would have read as follows:

Dear Jesus of Nazareth,

Thank you for entrusting our firm to perform the psychological profiles on the men you have selected to lead your ministry. After careful evaluation, we have come to the following conclusions:

Simon Peter exhibits bipolar tendencies. If incited, his behavior may culminate in fits of rage inflicting harm on others. James and John are highly competitive and self-centered and will most likely attempt a hostile takeover of your organization. Thomas is self-doubting, uncertain, and lacks confidence, while

Matthew has been barred from the Merchant Men's Fellowship of Greater Jerusalem.

Upon close examination, we have determined that if you do not reconsider these choices, your ministerial vision to evangelize the world will not succeed.

Despite these flaws, Jesus looked at His twelve ragged, principally uneducated, imperfect followers and spoke this blessing: "You are the salt of the earth and the light of the world."

They received Christ's blessing in faith and acted upon it. At that exact moment they were nothing, but they rose to the level of accomplishment spoken by Jesus in His Prophetic Blessing, and they went out and shook the world.

✟ ✟ ✟

When I taught the power of the Prophetic Blessing to my congregation, I directed every father or mother to lay hands on his or her children and speak a blessing over them. I instructed them to personally profess the future accomplishments they desired for each child. Lives were immediately changed. Weeping could be heard from every corner of the sanctuary. Testimonies began pouring in of sons and daughters whose lives were transformed by the power of the Prophetic Blessing spoken over them by their spiritual authority. School grades improved; behavioral problems and low self-esteem vanished! Their children walked and talked with an air of confidence they had never demonstrated before.

❡ THINK on THIS ❡

The supernatural Prophetic Blessing is invoked by speaking aloud. Once the blessing has been spoken, it cannot be rescinded. When God Almighty, King of the universe, places His blessing upon you, no person on earth can take it from you, and no power in the universe can eliminate it from your life!

The power of the Prophetic Blessing has changed the course of our ministry and positively impacted our congregation, our nation, and the nations of the world with supernatural results that were beyond our most aspiring dreams or imagination.

Chapter Two

BORN TO BE BLESSED

And the Lord spoke to Moses, saying: "Speak to Aaron and his sons, saying, 'This is the way you shall bless the children of Israel. Say to them:

"The Lord bless you and keep you;
The Lord make His face shine upon you,
And be gracious to you;
The Lord lift up His countenance upon you,
And give you peace."'

"So they shall put My name on the children of Israel, and I will bless them."

—Numbers 6:22–27

I have been in the ministry for more than fifty-four years, and I presently pastor a congregation of more than twenty thousand active members. I talk to people every day who feel helpless, hopeless, and worthless. They truly believe their lives have little meaning and direction; ultimately, they are living unhappy and unblessed lives.

I counsel with disillusioned businessmen who look into their financial futures and see national and global economic chaos and desolation. I listen to disheartened wives who feel their marriages have lost their passion and purpose. I sympathize with discouraged college graduates who cannot find jobs even though they are highly qualified. I attempt to encourage dejected single mothers who are working hard to raise their children, who want desperately to find a godly husband, but who feel an unseen power is taking their lives in a downward spiral.

I have a message of hope and truth for my congregation and for everyone reading this book who wants to live a fulfilled and successful life: God Almighty has declared that every one of His children is *born to be blessed*!

Read aloud the profoundly transforming promises from God to you in the Priestly Blessing:

And the Lord spoke to Moses, saying: "Speak to Aaron and his sons, saying, 'This is the way you shall bless the children of Israel. Say to them:

"The LORD bless you and keep you;
The LORD make His face shine upon you,
And be gracious to you;
The LORD lift up His countenance upon you,
And give you peace."'
"So they shall put My name on the children of Israel,
and I will bless them." (Numbers 6:22–27)

Did you take in the assurances uttered by God: "bless you and keep you"? Read the last four words of this blessing: who is The *Name* that has promised to bless you?

It is not Warren Buffet or Donald Trump! It is not the lottery commissioner informing you that you have just won a multimillion-dollar prize. It is not your rich aunt's estate or the latest bailout program from Washington, DC. Who is The *Name*?

The name Rockefeller will open the doors of finance, the name Einstein will open the doors of science, and the name Beethoven will open the doors of music halls around the world—but it is The *Name* of the Lord that opens the doors of heaven and blesses you with blessings you cannot contain!

This awesome promise can only come from an awesome God. This blessing is coming to *you* directly from the Creator of heaven and earth. The prophet Isaiah called Him "Wonderful, Counselor, Mighty God, Everlasting Father, Prince of Peace" (Isaiah 9:6). Sacred Scripture calls Him the great "I AM," the Great Physician, and the "Good Shepherd" of the sheep (Exodus 3:14; Luke 5:31; John 10:11).

The mighty source of blessing that knows no limit is Emmanuel, God with us, and the hope of glory. He is the immortal and invisible God. He can restore your dead marriage, heal your diseased body, and renew your distressed mind. He has promised to make you the head and not the tail. He will give you houses you didn't build, vineyards you didn't plant, and wells you didn't dig. He will plant you by rivers of living water, and whatsoever you do will prosper! He is the Lord who gives you the power to get wealth.

I want you, regardless of your circumstances or how hopeless you may feel at this very moment, to say aloud, "I was born to be blessed!"

Begin thinking of yourself as successful in everything you put your hand to. I encourage you to end all destructive speech about yourself, your spouse, your children, your current circumstances, and your future.

You have the power to turn your life around! You must confront yourself in the mirror and declare that you will no longer accept a mediocre existence for yourself or your loved ones.

✢ THINK on THIS ✢

You cannot change what you will not confront!
You have the ability, through the power of the blessing,
to revolutionize your life and control your future.

You don't need to search any further for the answers to the challenges of your life; you just need to believe that you have the potential to lead a blessed life . . . because you were *born to be blessed*!

THE BLESSING DEFINED

When we encounter a stranger who sneezes in the elevator, most of us instinctively say, "God bless you!" There is an Irish blessing that states: "May you be in heaven thirty minutes before the devil knows you're dead." A Hispanic farewell proclaims a blessing for a safe journey through the phrase "*Vaya con Dios.*" Even Boaz of the Old Testament greeted his reapers with a blessing: "The Lord be with you" (Ruth 2:4).

There are many ways man desires to extend his blessing upon others. These kinds of statements may seek God's favor upon something or someone; however, they are not examples of the God-ordained Priestly Blessing, nor are they an impartation of the Prophetic Blessing. Let us begin by defining the difference between the Priestly Blessing and the Prophetic Blessing.

THE PRIESTLY BLESSING

The book of Numbers houses within its pages what is often referred to as the Lord's Prayer of the Old Testament. The Lord commanded Moses to instruct Aaron and his sons to bless the children of Israel by placing His Name upon them. Aaron and his sons comprised the priesthood of Israel, and therefore this passage is referred to as the Priestly Blessing.

This profound proclamation is one of God's gifts to His own, for within its sacred text He defines the essence of the word *blessing*. In reading its promises, we can look into the heart of God and experience a small portion of the great love He has for us.

THE CONTENT OF THE PRIESTLY BLESSING

⋎ THINK ON THIS ⋎

The Priestly Blessing belongs to God; its words can never be altered in any way as declared in Proverbs 30:6: "Do not add to His words, lest He rebuke you, and you be found a liar."

The Priestly Blessing was not just for Moses, Aaron, and the elite members of the tribe of Levi; it was intended for *every person on the face of the earth.*

The verb *to bless* in Hebrew is related to the noun *knee* and can mean "to adore on bended knee" (Psalm 95:6) or "to present something of value to another." Nearly every Hebrew blessing begins with this word, for God deserves all of man's praise and adoration (Psalm 113:2). Through the Priestly Blessing, God is bestowing His favor on *His* creation—mortal man. How humbling! This is the purest expression of His mercy and grace.[1] God blesses His children by giving us life and provision; we bless Him through our praise and by living our lives to the fullest.

⚜ THINK on THIS ⚜

If you enjoy something in the world without saying a blessing, it is as if you stole it. — The Talmud

Let us briefly study the meaning of the promises God makes within the Priestly Blessing to give you a better understanding of their potentially profound effect on your life and the lives of those you love.

The Priestly Blessing is composed of three major promises and each promise has two parts.

1. The First Promise: "The LORD bless you and keep you."
In the Hebrew, the first sentence is three words long and captures God's guarantee of abundant life for the righteous. God's blessings upon His children are countless and personal (Deuteronomy 7:12–16). Jesus echoed this truth when He said, "Seek first the kingdom of God and His righteousness, and *all these things shall be added to you*" (Matthew 6:33).

The first part of the first promise, *bless you*, declares God's goodness. This promise invokes the favor of God without limit, which includes physical (Psalm 103:2-3; Isaiah 53:5; Matthew 4:23; Luke 9:11; Acts 10:38), emotional (Psalm 55:18; Isaiah

26:3, 61:1; John 14:27; 2 Timothy 1:6-8), relational (Psalm 133; 1 John 1:7), and material abundance (Genesis 30:30 AMP; Deuteronomy 8:18; 2 Chronicles 1:12; Proverbs 8:21; Ecclesiastes 5:19; Malachi 3:10; 1 Corinthians 3:7). The second part of the first promise, *keep you*, states that God will not only bestow His unmerited favor upon you; He will also protect you and the many blessings He has imparted upon you.[2]

❧ THINK ON THIS ❧

God is watching over you. "For He shall give His angels charge over you, to keep you in all your ways" (Psalm 91:11).

The president of the United States has highly trained Secret Service agents who protect him and his family day and night. Like the president, you as a believer are not alone. You are assisted and defended by a powerful and glorious order of invisible beings. God's "secret agents" are watching over you and every member of your family.

God promises to "guard and protect," and we in turn are to "keep [His] covenant" (Exodus 19:5–7) by loving Him and keeping His commandments (Exodus 20:6).[3]

2. The Second Promise: "The Lord make His face shine upon you, and be gracious to you."

The first part of the second promise is five words long in the Hebrew language and is a blessing for spiritual growth.[4]

What does it mean to have one's face shine? The Hebrew verb for *shine* in this text means "to shed light or illuminate," or to "become light."[5] Jewish scholars better define this phrase by studying the opposite meaning, "to hide one's face," as demonstrated in Deuteronomy 31:18 when God refers to the curses over those who worshiped other gods—"I will surely hide My face [from them]"—or in Psalm 88:14, when David cries out to God and asks, "Why do You hide Your face from me?"

For God to hide His face means He is showing His wrath, chastisement, and rejection; ultimately it means to have God remove His presence from you (1 Samuel 28:15). On the other hand, to have God "shine His face" upon you means to dwell in the presence of God. What a remarkable thought! Dwelling in God's presence can be seen throughout Scripture (Psalm 68:2; Zephaniah 1:7; Luke 1:19; Romans 4:17; Hebrews 9:24).

Believers dwell with God by abiding in and obeying His Word: "For the commandment is a lamp, and the law a light" (Proverbs 6:23). Therefore, our lives are illuminated by the wisdom found in the Word of God; it is a "lamp to my feet and a light to my path" (Psalm 119:105).

The second part of this promise, "and be gracious to you," translates in the Hebrew to mean "to show favor" or "to be gracious toward." There are two very significant certainties within this phrase: first, man cannot demand God's presence, and second, in His sovereignty, God chooses to whom He will reveal His presence.[6]

God's infinite grace is displayed in the fact that He sent His Son to dwell among us. Through Christ, God the Father reveals Himself: "For it is the God who commanded light to shine out of darkness, who has shone in our hearts to give the light of the knowledge of the glory of God in the face of Jesus Christ" (2 Corinthians 4:6). Furthermore, Jesus Christ referred to the Priestly Blessing when He called His followers the "light of the world" (Matthew 5:14).

3. The Third Promise: "The LORD lift up His countenance upon you, and give you peace."

The first part of this portion of the blessing is seven words long in Hebrew and conveys God's approval. When man is petitioning a request, he lifts up his face toward the one granting the request; but in this case, it is the Lord who will "lift up His countenance [or face]" upon His people. In the Hebrew figure of speech, it is simply defined as "God will smile upon you."[7]

The second part within this promise refers to *shalom*, or peace. *Peace* is defined in the natural as the absence of war or struggle; however, in the supernatural element of the Priestly Blessing, the word *shalom* means "to be finished or completed"; it is "harmony between conflicting forces."[8] Therefore, the Father's peace is "whole, it surpasses understanding and it lacks nothing."[9]

When a parent smiles upon his or her child, it brings the child comfort, confidence, approval, and ultimately peace.

Likewise, when our heavenly Father smiles upon His children, it too produces a sense of security, acceptance, and wholeness; but more importantly, with God's peace you can enjoy the other promises of the Priestly Blessing, which are provision and protection, wisdom, redemption, and favor.

The first promise of the Priestly Blessing is three Hebrew words in length. The second promise is five words in length, but the third promise of the Priestly Blessing is composed of seven Hebrew words.[10]

In the Bible, the number seven represents perfection or completeness. This portion of the Prophetic Blessing declares that without peace you have nothing, no matter how wealthy, wise, or socially connected you may be.

St. Paul recognized the promises of grace and peace within the Priestly Blessing to be essential ingredients in living the good life, for he began all but one of his epistles with the words: "Grace to you and peace from God our Father and the Lord Jesus Christ."

This confirms that any blessing is incomplete unless it brings with it peace. To be truly blessed with material provision, scholarly wisdom, and spiritual gain requires the gift of peace.

⅋ THINK ON THIS ⅋

Without the peace of God there is no blessing![11]

INVOKING THE NAME OF GOD

In the final portion of the Priestly Blessing (Numbers 6:27), the Lord instructs Aaron and his sons to invoke His Name on the children of Israel so that God Himself could sanctify Israel with the holiness that is embodied by The *Name*. Only then would the people be worthy of His blessing. This was a reminder that even though the priests pronounced the words of the blessing, only God can bless.[12]

The *Name* reveals the one true God. He is the *One Who Was, Is,* and *Is to Come*. He is the God through whom all things have their existence (1 Corinthians 8:6). Therefore, by placing His Name upon His children, God reminds us of who He is, which defines His character; of what He has done, which declares His mighty works; and of what He promises to do, which proclaims His covenant. Ultimately this decree underscores that God and God alone is the source of all blessings in every realm of life. To accept this truth demands the purest of faith, which is the conduit for God's blessing.[13]

THE PROPHETIC BLESSING

Let us now briefly distinguish between the Priestly Blessing and the Prophetic Blessing. While the Priestly Blessing is *God's* direct proclamation over man as stated in Numbers 6, the Prophetic Blessing is the spoken declaration by God's *spiritual authority* concerning the life of an individual. Once the Priestly Blessing has been spoken over the recipient, then the Prophetic Blessing follows. Unlike the Priestly Blessing, the Prophetic Blessing is unique to every person imparting it as well as to the one receiving it. *"And he blessed them; he blessed each one according to his own blessing"* (Genesis 49:28).

The scriptural reference to the word *blessing* has several connotations in the Hebrew language. When God blesses man, it is to bestow good health, abundant success, and prosperity, both materially and spiritually. When man blesses God, it is presented in the forms of thanksgiving, reverence, obedience, praise, and worship. When a man blesses his fellow believer, he recites the Priestly Blessing of Numbers 6:22–27 and then proclaims the Holy Spirit-inspired Prophetic Blessing.

As you read *The Power of the Prophetic Blessing,* you will discover how this divine proclamation, guided by the Holy Spirit, will supernaturally form your life and the lives of those you love.

Chapter Three

THE GENESIS BLESSING

So God created man in His own image; in the image of God
He created him; male and female He created them.

—Genesis 1:27

The word *created* in Hebrew is *bara*, meaning "to make from nothing." Before Creation, there was nothing apart from the glory of God. Just as the blind cannot comprehend the majesty of the sunset or the deaf the beauty of a symphony, man cannot conceive the concept of the term *nothing*.[1] Before the sun and the moon, before light and darkness, there was only God. God the Almighty—the Alpha and Omega . . . the Great I AM.

In the book of Genesis He is the Seed of the Woman. In the book of Exodus He is our Passover Lamb. In the book of

Ruth He is our Kinsman Redeemer. In the book of Psalms He is our Shepherd. In the book of Isaiah He is our Prince of Peace. In the book of John He is the Son of God. In the book of Acts He is the Holy Ghost. In the book of Hebrews He is the Blood of the Everlasting Covenant. In the book of James He is the Great Physician. And in the book of Revelation He is the King of kings and Lord of lords![2]

⅄ THINK ON THIS ⅄

From nothing (bara) the Master Architect of the Ages created the universe and everything in it using His Spoken Word as His blueprint! "And God said . . ."

THE CREATION OF ADAM

In the theater of your mind, stand with me in the Garden of Eden and witness God Almighty kneeling on the ground as He scoops up a handful of dirt. The Creator of all life is molding in His majestic hands the first human being, called *Adam*. "And the LORD God formed man of the dust of the ground" (Genesis 2:7).

This mortal temple of clay lay lifeless in the shadows of Eden until God pressed His face against Adam's and breathed into him: "And [God] breathed into his nostrils the breath of life; and man became a living being" (Genesis 2:7).

My dear friends, Adam did not evolve; he was wondrously and marvelously made by the perfect hands of the Potter just as you and I were made. King David put pen to parchment and wrote, "I am fearfully and wonderfully made" (Psalm 139:14). My dear friends, we were *all* created . . . we did not evolve!

When Adam first opened his eyes to the light of day, he was awed by both the majesty and tranquility of the Garden of Eden. The duet of the Creator and the created spoke to each other as they walked down the lush green paths of the garden. Then the Lord gave His tenth command of Genesis: "It is not good that man should be alone; I will make him a helper comparable to him" (2:18).

THE CREATION OF EVE

Much has been said about Eve, including the following tale:

God said to Adam, "I'm going to create for you a wife who will love you no matter what you do—a wife who will cook three delicious meals each day for you; she will wash and mend your clothes; she will make passionate love to you whenever you want; she will bear your children without complaint; and she will always agree with you no matter what."

Adam asked the Lord, "And how much will a wife like that cost?"

The Lord responded, "It will cost you an arm and a leg."

Adam thought for a moment and asked, "And what can I get for a rib?"

The Lord God, the Great Physician, performed the first surgery in human history; God was both anesthesiologist and surgeon. He placed Adam in a deep sleep, split his side, and extracted a rib from which He created the most beautiful and mysterious creature the world would ever know—woman.

Matthew Henry said that "woman was made of a rib out of the side of Adam; not made out of his head to rule over him, nor out of his feet to be trampled on by him, but out of his side to be equal with him, but under his arm to be protected, and near his heart to be beloved."[3]

ᛦ THINK ON THIS ᛦ

Marriage is God's idea; man had no part in planning it.
It is and will remain the cornerstone of civilization.

As we witness the first marriage, Eve—the essence of absolute perfection—is presented to her husband by the ultimate Matchmaker, the Father of all creation.

To further consecrate this union, God bestowed His blessing.

A THREEFOLD BLESSING

The Lord did not create the earth to be a wasteland: He formed it to be inhabited.[4] "For thus says the LORD, who created the heavens, who is God, who formed the earth and made it, who has established it, who did not create it in vain, who formed it to be inhabited: 'I am the LORD, and there is no other'" (Isaiah 45:18).

The first blessing over man and woman in Scripture is recorded in Genesis 1:28: "Then God blessed them, and God said to them, 'Be fruitful and multiply; fill the earth and subdue it; have dominion over the fish of the sea, over the birds of the air, and over every living thing that moves on the earth.'"

The threefold cord of the Genesis Blessing includes:

1. Be fruitful and multiply.
2. Fill the earth and subdue it.
3. Have dominion over all things.

BE FRUITFUL AND MULTIPLY

"Be fruitful and multiply" is both a blessing and a command. The union of one man with one woman is intended to produce children. This command is the antithesis of the pro-abortion and pro-homosexual agenda. It is not possible for two men or two women to produce a child. God created "male and female," making marriage between two men or two women a clear violation of the law of God. God will only bless the union He created; therefore He blessed the union of marriage between a man and a woman with children, as recorded by King David in Psalm 127:3–5:

Children are a heritage from the LORD,
The fruit of the womb is a reward.
Like arrows in the hand of a warrior,
So are the children of one's youth.
Happy is the man who has his quiver full of them;
They shall not be ashamed,
But shall speak with their enemies in the gate.

America does not treat our children as rewards or respect them for the blessing God intended them to be. They are instead exploited through child pornography, abused through neglect, and killed through abortion. Because of these transgressions, a portion of our nation's future has been destroyed. Since *Roe v. Wade*, more than fifty-three million children have been murdered in the wombs of their mothers.[5]

A potential Mozart, an Einstein, a future president of the United States, schoolteachers, firefighters, police officers, loving mothers, and compassionate fathers have been eliminated from our society because we have failed to honor God's command to be fruitful and multiply. The most endangered species on earth is a child in the womb of his or her mother.

⚡ THINK ON THIS ⚡

Had the mothers of ancient Israel killed the children in their wombs, the Lord's divine destiny for man would have been aborted. There would have been no Abraham, Isaac, or Jacob. There would have been no prophets of Israel to bring the guiding light of truth to future generations. There would have been no King David, who destroyed the enemies of Israel, and there would have been no miraculous birth in the manger of Bethlehem that changed the destiny of all mankind. God's plan of redemption would have been sacrificed on the altar of the god of self.

GOD KNEW ESAU AND JACOB

God performed a divine sonogram on the womb of Rebekah, who was concerned about the condition of her pregnancy and asked, as many expectant mothers have throughout recorded history, "If all is well, why am I like this?" (Genesis 25:22).

The Almighty read the sonogram of the children in Rebekah's womb and gave this prophetic proclamation:

> *Two nations are in your womb,*
> *Two peoples shall be separated from your body;*
> *One people shall be stronger than the other,*
> *And the older [Esau] shall serve the younger [Jacob].*
> *(Genesis 25:23)*

When God looked into Rebekah's womb, He did not see a blob of meaningless, lifeless flesh; He saw two living human beings. He gave a prophetic proclamation that Jacob and his descendants, the Jewish people, would be stronger than his brother, Esau, and his descendants.

Jacob, the heel catcher, was a rascal who knew the power of the blessing and used his craft and cunning to deceptively obtain it from his aged father, Isaac. Esau foolishly relinquished his right to the blessing for a bowl of beans and suffered greatly for it. God never forgot Esau's mockery of the blessing, for His words of anger still cut like a knife: "Jacob I have loved, but Esau I have hated" (Romans 9:13).

God the Father knew Jacob's destiny and He called it forth as He spoke a Prophetic Blessing over him: "Then God appeared to Jacob again, when he came from Padan Aram, and blessed him. And God said to him, 'Your name is Jacob; your name shall not be called Jacob anymore, but Israel shall be your name.' So He called his name Israel. Also, God said to him: "'I am God Almighty. Be fruitful and multiply; a nation and a company of nations shall proceed from you, and kings shall come for your body. The land which I gave Abraham and Isaac I give to you; and to your descendants after you I give this land'" (Genesis 35:9-12).

GOD KNEW JEREMIAH

Jeremiah, the weeping prophet, was known to God *before he was born* as a person with a specific destiny. Here is God's prophetic proclamation concerning Jeremiah's sonogram:

Then the word of the LORD came to me, saying:
"Before I formed you in the womb I knew you;
Before you were born I sanctified you;
I ordained you a prophet to the nations." (Jeremiah 1:4–5)

This verse clearly declares three things:

1. God knew your child before he or she was conceived in the womb.
2. God has called children to a divine work and has sanctified them for that work while they were in their mothers' wombs. Remember, John the Baptist leaped in his mother's womb because he was filled with the Holy Ghost.
3. God ordained Jeremiah as a prophet to the nations of the world. This divine destiny was determined before he breathed his first breath outside his mother's body.

⅋ THINK ON THIS ⅋

God spoke the Prophetic Blessing over His creation,
and He wants you to speak it over your children as well.

GOD KNEW JOHN THE BAPTIST

Zacharias was an elderly priest in Israel who was married to a woman named Elizabeth. They had no children because Elizabeth was barren, and they were both well advanced in years.

Zacharias went to the temple to serve his rotation, as was the custom of the priesthood. While he was praying, the angel Gabriel appeared to him saying:

> *Do not be afraid, Zacharias, for your prayer is heard; and your wife Elizabeth will bear you a son, and you shall call his name John. And you will have joy and gladness, and many will rejoice at his birth. For he will be great in the sight of the Lord, and shall drink neither wine nor strong drink. He will also be filled with the Holy Spirit, even from his mother's womb. And he will turn many of the children of Israel to the Lord their God. He will also go before Him in the spirit and power of Elijah, "to turn the hearts of the fathers to the children," and the disobedient to the wisdom of the just, to make ready a people prepared for the Lord. (Luke 1:13–17)*

The angel of the Lord gave Zacharias the exact details about the life and future ministry of the child in the womb of Elizabeth. He also declared that John the Baptist would be filled with the Holy Spirit in the womb of his mother.

Only a human being can have a supernatural experience, not a blob of flesh.

Diana and I are the proud parents of five wonderful children and twelve amazing grandchildren who are the joy of our lives. We can undeniably state that they are God's greatest blessing to us.

GOD KNEW MATTHEW

When I sit on the platform of Cornerstone Church and watch our son Matthew preaching to our congregation and television audience that reaches across the nation and around the world, it's all I can do to keep myself from jumping to my feet and shouting for joy. He is an answer to prayer—and Satan tried to kill him while he was in his mother's womb.

Diana and I were thrilled when the doctor confirmed she was pregnant with Matthew. A few weeks after the news of her pregnancy, Diana ministered to a young girl in our church who was not feeling well. The following day the girl's mother called to inform Diana that the doctor diagnosed her daughter's condition over the phone as German measles. When Diana called her obstetrician to report that she had been exposed to German measles, he reviewed Diana's records and concluded that she had never had the measles nor had she ever received the immunization against the virus.

The doctor proceeded to inform Diana that the German measles, medically known as rubella, can cause deformity and severe brain damage to a child in the mother's womb.

Diana was in shock but was somewhat relieved when she heard her doctor softly say, "Don't worry, we can take care of everything with one visit to the office."

Diana asked what his plan for treatment was. His answer: "It's a simple in-office procedure called dilation and curettage, or a D&C. It's an easy procedure that can be done in less than an hour." In other words . . . an abortion!

Diana hung up the phone and turned pale as tears started streaming down her face. She had attended the university as a premed student and knew instantly we were in a crisis of faith.

Diana called my office, crying, as she related to me the doctor's plan to terminate her pregnancy.

"What are we going to do?" she sobbed into the phone.

"Step one: fire the doctor! We're going to trust God that the life in your body will be born perfectly healthy and fulfill the divine destiny God has already charted!"

I immediately called the doctor and dismissed him. Before we hung up, he gave me the "irresponsible person" speech, trying to manipulate me with guilt to terminate the pregnancy. He failed!

When Diana arrived at my office, her eyes were swollen from crying. She sat down in a chair across from my desk, looked me straight in the eye, and said, "Now what?"

What do you do when you don't know what to do? You do exactly this: "Trust in the LORD with all your heart, and lean not on your own understanding; *in all your ways* acknowledge

Him, and He shall direct your paths" (Proverbs 3:5–6). We cried in each other's arms, proclaimed a healthy pregnancy and delivery, and then waited on God.

Are you ready for this?

Three days later, the woman who had called Diana to report that her daughter had German measles called again. She told Diana, "I wanted to follow up with you on the condition of our daughter. She began to improve much quicker than the doctor had predicted, so I took her into his office where he confirmed that he had misdiagnosed her; it was only a skin rash of some kind, not the German measles."

Diana began to weep again, out of gratitude and relief, but also out of anguish as her mind fell on the unthinkable: had we followed the advice of our doctor, Matthew never would have been born.

Matthew's birth was the first that I was allowed to witness by the hospital. I saw him take his first breath. I was the first to hold him. As I held our healthy miracle baby in my arms, he smiled his first smile, and I wept for joy. Had Matthew's life been taken in his mother's womb, the Lord's divine destiny for him would have been aborted.

I am the fifth consecutive generation in the Hagee family to become a pastor; our son Matthew continues this revered heritage as the sixth generation to preach the gospel of Jesus Christ. Diana and I are praying that one of his sons will continue the legacy of the Hagee family.

I thank You, Lord, for the revelation truth of Your precious

Word: "I have come that they may have life, and that they may have it more abundantly" (John 10:10).

FILL THE EARTH

The second blessing of the threefold cord is to "fill the earth and subdue it" (Genesis 1:28). God, the Father of all Creation, the Sovereign King of the universe, could have populated the earth with one prophetic proclamation after He created Adam—but He didn't. Not because He couldn't, but because He wanted man to accomplish the task. God planned for man to propagate the whole earth.

In Genesis 1:28, God commanded Adam to "fill the earth," and again He instructed Noah in Genesis 9:1: "So God blessed Noah and his sons, and said to them: 'Be fruitful and multiply, and fill the earth.'" When man refuses to obey God's mandate, the Almighty takes matters into His own hands to accomplish that which He has decreed. For instance, mankind united to build a city in the plains of Shinar for the purpose of personal glory: "Come, let us build ourselves a city, with a tower that reaches to the heavens, so that we may make a name for ourselves *and not be scattered over the face of the whole earth*" (Genesis 11:4 NIV1984).

In blatant rebellion, man defied God's command to "fill the earth," so God thwarted man's plan by confusing the language and setting them on the path He had originally ordained through the Genesis Blessing: "So the LORD scattered them abroad from there over the face of all the earth" (Genesis 11:8).

❦ THINK on THIS ❦

Where God plants you is where He will bless you and provide for you. The place of His purpose is the place of His power!

Had Elijah not gone to the Brook Cherith as God commanded, he would have been without protection and would have eventually starved to death. "Get away from here and turn eastward, and hide by the Brook Cherith, which flows into the Jordan. And it will be that you shall drink from the brook, and I have commanded the ravens to feed you there" (1 Kings 17:3–4).

Had the apostles not gone back to Jerusalem as commanded by Christ, they would never have received the infilling of the Holy Spirit in the Upper Room. They would have remained simple fishermen reminiscing about missed opportunities. Instead, they obeyed the Lord and eventually, under the anointing of the Holy Spirit, turned the world upside down with the good news of the gospel.

And being assembled together with them, [Jesus] commanded them not to depart from Jerusalem, but to wait for the Promise of the Father . . . "you shall be baptized with the Holy Spirit not many days from now. You shall receive power when the Holy Spirit has come upon you; and you shall be witnesses to Me in Jerusalem, and in all

Judea and Samaria, and to the end of the earth." (Acts 1:4–5, 8)

SUBDUE

The word *subdue* within the Genesis Blessing means "to master or care for." From the beginning, the "untamed natural creation was to be ordered by human intelligence and will. This was not an invitation to exploit the creation; it was a challenge to bring order and harmony to the physical earth."[6]

Adam and Eve were to use all the infinite resources of the earth in the service of God and man. Remember, sin had not yet entered mankind, therefore Adam and Eve's role as caretakers of the Garden was without strife, resistance, or death; man was forbidden to kill animals for food. (Such permission was granted to Noah after the flood [Genesis 9:3].) Instead their lives were pleasant, successful, and gratifying.

This Genesis blessing is *still* intended for us; we *can* have pleasant, successful, and gratifying lives through the Second Adam, Jesus Christ our Savior.

HAVE DOMINION

Man was made in God's image; we are His image-bearers, therefore we hold the attributes of God within us. God's intent for man was to be king (to take control) over nature on His behalf, treating it as He would (Genesis 1:28). This command hits the twenty-first century like a sledgehammer between the eyes.

The basis of neo-pagan environmentalism is the worship of nature; it elevates animals and Mother Earth over the rights of human beings. Many of the people who demand the protection of whales or blind beetles are the same who clamor for on-demand abortion. Those who are concerned for the continuation of endangered species should also be concerned for the rights of the unborn child—a true endangered species.

The other side of the coin is this: mankind has desecrated much of God's creation through disregard and misuse. Through the Genesis Blessing, man is to take control of nature, but it forbids cruelty and selfish abuse. As God's image-bearers we should exercise dominion with His character.

When Jesus Christ was on the earth, He had total dominion over every living thing. In Luke 5, Jesus told His disciples to launch out into the deep for a catch, and they caught so many fish it almost sank their boats (vv. 4–7). In Matthew 17, Jesus told Peter to go fishing and catch only one fish, which would have money in its mouth to pay their taxes (v. 27). That's absolute control!

Jesus had dominion over an unbroken colt when He rode into Jerusalem through wildly cheering crowds who were waving palm branches on every side, shouting, "Hosanna!"

Jesus demonstrated control over the fowl of the air when the cock crowed twice immediately after Peter denied knowing Him for the third time.

Jesus had control of the elements when He commanded water to become the finest wine at the wedding in Cana.

I ask you this question: If God gave dominion over nature to Adam and to Jesus, why is our generation idolizing what God says we should control?

Adam dwelled serenely in the Garden of Eden as a result of his obedience to God's commandments, and he protected that blessed existence by avoiding transgression. Mankind received the Genesis Blessing through Adam, and even though Adam succumbed to sin, God—through His mercy and grace—provides the opportunity for each of His children to benefit from the Genesis Blessing.

We are now about to embark to Ur to meet a man named Abram, who was given the Eternal Covenant through the Abrahamic Blessing, a blessing that can also be yours: "I will bless those who bless you."

CHAPTER FOUR

THE ABRAHAMIC BLESSING

Now the L<small>ORD</small> had said to Abram:
"Get out of your country,
From your family
And from your father's house,
To a land that I will show you.
I will make you a great nation;
I will bless you
And make your name great."

—G<small>ENESIS</small> 12:1–2

It was God's call to Jacob at Bethel that transformed him from a man who was running from his past to a man named Israel, who saw the Almighty face-to-face: "For you have struggled with God and with men, and have prevailed" (Genesis 32:28).

It was the call of God that sent the prophet Samuel with his oil-filled horn to anoint a shepherd boy as king: "Now the LORD said to Samuel, 'How long will you mourn for Saul, seeing I have rejected him from reigning over Israel? Fill your horn with oil, and go'" (1 Samuel 16:1).

It was the call of God that sent David to kill Goliath, to conquer the Jebusites, and to liberate the city of Jerusalem, which became the eternal and undivided capital of Israel forever.

It was the call of God upon Saul of Tarsus, a man named after the first king of Israel who changed the face of Christianity. Saul guarded the garments of the men who stoned Stephen to death. He terrorized the New Testament church by sending some of its followers to prison and others to execution. And then he was smitten to the ground by a divine arrest warrant, with Jesus asking him, "Saul, Saul, why are you persecuting Me? . . . Arise and go into the city, and you will be told what you must do" (Acts 9:4, 6).

It was John the Revelator, imprisoned on the isle of Patmos as an enemy of Rome, who heard the call from heaven sounding like a trumpet: "Come up here, and I will show you things which must take place after this" (Revelation 4:1).

Soon the bride of Christ, from every kindred, tongue, and tribe, will hear the call of God as the trumpet sounds: "The dead in Christ will rise first. Then we who are alive and remain shall be caught up together with them in the clouds to meet the Lord in the air. And thus we shall always be with the Lord" (1 Thessalonians 4:16–17).

When the call of God comes to mortal flesh, there is no need for announcement; for men can feel it, angels celebrate it, and demons scatter in terror.

I am asked repeatedly by young men and women who aspire to the ministry, "What is the first thing I must do?"

The answer is this: Wait for the call of God. When *His call* comes, it will be like a fire in your bones, a fire you will not be able to contain or quench. But until that time comes, all mortal activity is but wasted motion.

The transformed St. Paul declared that we are called "with a holy calling, not according to our works, but according to His own purpose and grace which was given to us in Christ Jesus before time began" (2 Timothy 1:9).

The difference between an idol worshiper in Mesopotamia named Abram and the father of many nations named Abraham was the *call of God*. With the call of God, nothing is impossible; without the call, you are as sounding brass and a clanging cymbal (1 Corinthians 13:1).

The call of God upon this man began with one simple statement of supernatural empowerment: "Now the Lord had said to Abram . . ." (Genesis 12:1). It was this divine call of Almighty God that set Abram apart to become not only the "father of many nations" (Romans 4:16–18) but also the "friend of God" (2 Chronicles 20:7).

ABRAHAM TESTED

From the moment God called Abram, He tested him. Life is full of tests; in fact, life itself is a test. Interlaced through our lives are times of joy and sadness, times of success and failure, and times of hope and desperation; and woven within all of life's tapestry are the tests of time.

Joseph sat in an Egyptian prison for years, discouraged over his shattered dreams. Yet in one day he went from Egypt's prison to Pharaoh's penthouse with unprecedented position and power because God was faithful to the Prophetic Blessing He had given Joseph years before (Genesis 41:40–43).

Daniel was tested by the king's steward with the rich foods of royalty for ten days but instead decided to consume only vegetables and water, and he came forth as God's champion. He was tested when he spent the night in a den of starving lions, listening to their deafening roars, and certain that his body would be ripped to shreds by the razor-sharp teeth in their powerful jaws. And for passing these tests of faith, God gave Daniel "understanding in all visions and dreams," which caused him to eventually be promoted by the king to a place of national prominence for the rest of his life (see the book of Daniel).

Are you going through a fiery trial? Prepare yourself, for you are next in line for a promotion on your job, a restored relationship, a long-awaited financial provision, or a miraculous healing. Listen to the encouraging words of St. Peter:

"Beloved, do not think it strange concerning the fiery trial which is to try you, as though some strange thing happened to you; but rejoice to the extent that you partake of Christ's sufferings, that when His glory is revealed, you may also be glad with exceeding joy" (1 Peter 4:12–13).

⅋ THINK ON THIS ⅋

The person going through the test of fire is one step closer to attaining God's destiny.

Life's tests will take you from the agony of the valley of the shadow of death to the ecstasy of the mountaintop. Tests will come, but Jehovah Jireh promises us triumph over them all, for He is the Consuming Fire who takes us through the trials of life that purge us from the moral and spiritual imperfections that hinder our blessed and victorious future.

Let us examine the ten tests of Abraham and how they connect to the promises of God in the Abrahamic Blessing. These tests were the path Abram had to walk before receiving the Prophetic Blessing of God.

With God's *call* came the tests, the Prophetic Blessing, and ultimately the covenant for the land of Israel. Abram received a directive that few would have answered, yet he trusted God and obeyed His voice: "Blessed is the man who trusts in God and who makes God the source of his trust" (Jeremiah 17:7 The Torah).

Now the LORD *had said to Abram:*
"Get out of your country,
From your family
And from your father's house,
To a land that I will show you.
I will make you a great nation;
I will bless you
And make your name great;
And you shall be a blessing.
I will bless those who bless you,
And I will curse him who curses you;
And in you all the families of the earth shall be blessed."
(Genesis 12:1–3)

What did Abram do when he heard the call? "So Abram departed as the LORD had spoken to him" (Genesis 12:4).

The First Test: Absolute Obedience

Blessings come to those who obey. Moses took his quill and scratched into parchment the most profound principles of blessing in Scripture: "Now it shall come to pass, if you diligently obey the voice of the LORD your God, to observe carefully all His commandments which I command you today, that the LORD your God will set you high above all nations of the earth. And all these blessings shall come upon you and overtake you, because you obey the voice of the LORD your God" (Deuteronomy 28:1–2).

⅋ THINK on THIS ⅋

It's not what you believe that makes your life great; it is what you obey—for obedience is better than sacrifice (1 Samuel 15:22).

Many *hear* the Word but few *obey* it. I hear people say, "I believe in God but . . ." Demons believe in God; they tremble at the mention of His name (James 2:19), but they don't obey! Do you?

We hear voices every day clamoring for us to go *this way* and *that way*, but there is only one voice we need to heed—the voice of God. Abram heard the voice of God—a voice he had never heard before. It was the voice of an unseen and unknown God, yet Abram obeyed.

Abram was an idol worshiper. He was surrounded by an ungodly and pagan society. Yet, on one day he heard a voice from heaven calling him to leave where he was and go to a land he had never seen for a destiny he could never have comprehended. And immediately Abram arose to obey the voice of the unseen God that had called him to change the history of the world.

The Second Test: Separate Yourself

In one sentence, God tested Abram by telling him to remove himself from idols and idolatry. Abram was a successful merchant in Ur, a thriving and progressive city in Mesopotamia.

Yet he obediently left Ur, his family, and his very comfortable life to settle in Canaan, which was inhabited by people considered to be barbaric heathens.

The first step in God's divine plan of redemption was the separation of His people from a corrupt and idolatrous society. God called Abram out from the pagan customs of the Mesopotamian world in which he had been brought up.

⅄ THINK on THIS ⅄

Separation from the world is the gateway to spiritual power and blessing. The man who walks with God always reaches his destination!

If a nation is to have the blessing of God, if a church is to have the blessing of God, if a believer is to have the blessing of God, then there must be separation from the world. The church or believer who is just like the world can do nothing *for* the world. Jesus said, "And everyone who has left houses or brothers or sisters or father or mother or wife or children or lands, for My name's sake, shall receive a hundredfold, and inherit eternal life" (Matthew 19:29).

Later, on his journey to receive his Prophetic Blessing, Abram was told by God to leave the land of Canaan and go to Egypt. Both times Abram walked away from anyone or anything keeping him from fulfilling his divine destiny.

Adam and Eve could not walk away from the seductive

serpent who enticed them to eat the forbidden fruit, and they lost Eden. Samson could not walk away from Delilah, who seductively lured him into revealing the secret to the anointing God had given him, and he lost his life. Judas could not walk away from thirty pieces of silver, and he lost his soul.

Is the Prince of Darkness tempting you with forbidden fruit to lure you away from your blessing? Be like Abram: walk away today!

⅋ THINK on THIS ⅋

What you are able to walk away from will
determine what God can bring you to!

God was preparing Abram for the next test, which would take him closer to the Prophetic Blessing of Eretz Israel (the land of Israel), for God never orders us out until He is ready to lead us in.

The Third Test: Sarai and Pharaoh

Abram encountered a severe famine in Canaan, which drove him to Egypt. As he sojourned in Egypt, his thoughts were on the Prophetic Blessing God had spoken over him. Where was the blessing of the land?

Abram was afraid for his life and that of his wife's while in Egypt. It was the custom for Pharaoh to take beautiful women into his palace to satisfy his momentary salacious passion: "So it was, when Abram came into Egypt, that the Egyptians saw the woman, that she was very beautiful. The princes of Pharaoh also saw her and commended her to Pharaoh. And the woman was taken to Pharaoh's house" (Genesis 12:14–15).

Abram convinced his wife, Sarai, to say that she was his sister, for she was indeed the daughter of his father, but not the daughter of his mother. He watched as Sarai, the love of his life, was taken away. Again, where was the blessing? Abram trusted that God would deliver them, and God remained faithful: "He permitted no man to do them wrong; yes, He rebuked kings for their sakes, saying, 'Do not touch My anointed ones'" (1 Chronicles 16:21–22).

When you are in the will of God, you are surrounded by an invisible host of angels who protect you day and night from every form of danger. If you remain faithful to God through the test, He will see to it that you are protected and delivered and that your enemies will be scattered before you.

The Fourth Test: The Four Kings

The next test came when Abram heard that Lot, his nephew, was taken captive in the siege of Sodom by four kings who had already destroyed twelve nations. Abram, with faith in God, executed the first IDF (Israeli Defense Forces) commando raid with only the 318 servants who had been born in his house.

Abram rescued Lot, bringing the spoils of war to the king

of Sodom, who offered them back to Abram. But Abram refused to accept them and said to the king of Sodom, "I have raised my hand to the LORD, God Most High, the Possessor of heaven and earth, that I will take nothing, from a thread to a sandal strap, and that I will not take anything that is yours, lest you should say, 'I have made Abram rich'" (Genesis 14:22–23).

Many times, Abram and his descendants would trust God to lead them to victory against overwhelming odds in their future battles for their national survival. The God who defended the land and the people then is the same God who defends the land of Israel and the Jewish people to this day and for all time. He is the Defender of Israel, who "shall neither slumber nor sleep" (Psalm 121:4). The enemies of Israel must recognize that there is a Spy in the sky; He is Jewish, and He will use His unlimited righteous might to assure that the Abrahamic Blessing endures through the ages until His Son, Jesus Christ, rules from Jerusalem as King of kings and Lord of lords.

When Moses and the Israelites left Egypt for the Promised Land, Pharaoh assembled six hundred of his choice chariots, his leading generals, and all his mighty army to utterly destroy the defenseless children of Israel. Moses trusted in God and proclaimed the victory, for he comforted the people with these words: "Do not be afraid. Stand still, and see the salvation of the LORD, which He will accomplish for you today. For the Egyptians whom you see today, you shall see again no more forever. The LORD will fight for you, and you shall hold your peace" (Exodus 14:13–14).

In parting the Red Sea, destroying Pharaoh's chariots, and drowning his army, the Lord stayed true to His promise: "So the LORD saved Israel that day out of the hand of the Egyptians, and Israel saw the Egyptians dead on the seashore. Thus Israel saw the great work which the LORD had done in Egypt; so the people feared the LORD, and believed the LORD and His servant Moses" (Exodus 14:30–31).

Gideon trusted God to intervene on his behalf and was able to subdue the siege of the Midianite and Amalekite oppression with only three hundred faithful men armed with broken pitchers, trumpets, and torches (Judges 7).

The Lord once again defeated Israel's enemies, giving Hezekiah the victory as Sennacherib led his Assyrian armies in what seemed to be an impossible conquest (2 Chronicles 32). Angels swept across the encampment of the Assyrian army sleeping in their tents and left 185,000 dead. After the stunning defeat, Sennacherib returned to Nineveh and went to worship his god, Nisroch. While there, his sons entered the temple and cut him down with the sword (2 Kings 19:35–37).

The Lord continues His miraculous defense of Israel to this day. Hours after Israel declared itself an independent state in May 1948, seven Arab nations—boasting that they would "push the Jews into the sea"—collaborated against the newborn nation in a battle known as Israel's War of Independence (May 14–June 11, 1948). At the end of the battle, the tiny nation, outnumbered 100 to 1, not only defeated its invaders but acquired more land than that which had already been granted in the 1947 UN partition plan.[1]

The commander of operations, Yigael Yadin, declared that Israel's victory over her enemies was a "miracle." The *Oxford Dictionary* defines the word *miracle* as: "a surprising and welcome event that is not explicable by natural or scientific laws and is therefore considered to be the work of a *divine agency*." Yes, history has recorded miracle after miracle during the decisive War of Independence. I will mention but a few to prove the point that God will defend Israel, and in doing so, He is guarding His Prophetic Blessing over Abraham, which is His eternal covenant for the land of Israel.

- *The Battle at Safed.* Near the Sea of Galilee, a small unit of Israeli soldiers defended their position against thousands of Arabs. Drastically outnumbered and low on supplies, the soldiers held fast when, out of nowhere, a desert storm erupted. Seizing the opportunity to distract the enemy, the Israeli warriors took their remaining gasoline and doused fifty empty oil drums, set them ablaze, and rolled them down the hill. A frightening illusion was created as the flaming barrels thunderously approached their target. Blinded by the sand of the storm, the terrified and confused Arabs fled the battle, convinced they were under attack by a mysterious weapon.[2]

- *The Battle at Degania.* In another incidence, Israeli soldiers found themselves at the point of defeat as they defended the oldest kibbutz in Israel while under siege by a Syrian convoy of two hundred armored vehicles, including forty-five tanks. Outnumbered and without armaments, the defenders of Israel were unable to block the enemy's advancement. The only heavy artillery available in all of Israel at the time were four howitzers similar to the weaponry used during the Franco-Prussian War of 1870. Lieutenant Colonel Moshe Dayan immediately ordered two of the antiquated weapons to be dismantled and rushed to his battlefront. The howitzers were reassembled at the exact moment the first Syrian tank rolled through the kibbutz's border. The Israeli forces fired and miraculously made a direct hit on the lead tank with one of the two archaic guns, which represented half of the artillery cache in all of Israel! Immediately, the Syrian troops retreated because they firmly believed that this pinpoint attack had to have come from the sophisticated arsenal that Israel must have possessed.[3]

- *The Battle at Galilee.* As Israeli replacements mobilized in twenty-four crudely equipped armored trucks and cars to relieve exhausted troops who were beset in battle, they took a wrong turn and crossed the border into Lebanon. Unexpectedly, they encountered a convoy that was supplying the Syrian army in Galilee with dozens of trucks of ammunition, artillery, and several armored vehicles. Startled, the Israelis hurriedly fired and hit the first truck, which was a tanker filled with gasoline. It exploded instantly and ignited the truck immediately behind it, which was laden with hand grenades. Rapidly repeating explosions were heard for miles around, terrifying the Syrians who fled for their lives. Later, the Israeli troops discovered that because of this miraculous surprise encounter, the Arab attackers fled Israel, believing that the Israeli army had invaded Lebanon.[4]

- *The Battle at Lydda.* The Gideon miracle was repeated in the liberation of the airport at Lydda. Sixteen Israelis disguised as Arabs secretly entered the city as seven thousand Arab troops prepared for attack. Once night fell, they infiltrated the Arab masses and generated a Gideon-like commotion, which brought chaos and bedlam, causing the Arab troops to attack one another and abort their siege.[5]

- *The Battle at Mushrafa.* Israel's Commander Yigael Yadin used the Torah (the first five books of the Jewish Bible) as his strategic war map to find an ancient biblical road that had been overlooked for centuries. After clearing the path, Yadin led his troops and armored vehicles through the dark of night to victory as they toppled the Egyptian's principal military base. This miraculous strategic conquest was one of the triggers that ended the 1948 war two weeks later.[6]

God's supernatural protection of Israel did not end with the war of 1948, nor did it end with the Six-Day War of 1967, the Yom Kippur War of 1973, or all the battles in between. And it will not end when the enemies of Israel rise up against her in the future, as prophesized by the psalmist: "They have taken crafty counsel against Your people, and consulted together against Your sheltered ones. They have said, 'Come, and let us cut them off from being a nation, that the name of Israel may be remembered no more'" (Psalm 83:3–4).

The prophet Ezekiel named the armies and nations that will attack Israel in the near future in an effort to wipe it off the map. It will be a massive land invasion led by Gog and Magog (Russia), who will lead Persia (Iran), Ethiopia (the Islamic African nations), Libya, and Togarmah (Turkey). This military armada will be so massive and overwhelming that the nations of the world will consider Israel utterly defeated before the war even starts.

There is, however, a problem with the evil plan of Israel's enemies. God Almighty, the Defender of Israel, is sitting in the heavens and will become so enraged "that My fury will show in My face" (Ezekiel 38:18). As soon as the feet of the invading army of millions touches the soil of Israel, God will release His fury and annihilate the enemies of Israel, as described by the prophet Ezekiel.

The Omnipresent God of Abraham, Isaac, and Jacob will allow confusion to control those armies as they fire their weapons of destruction against one another (Ezekiel 38:21). God has promised to "rain down flooding rain, great hailstones, fire, and brimstone [on the invading armies]" (Ezekiel 38:22). This is exactly how the Almighty destroyed Sodom and Gomorrah. How many of the invading army will be destroyed? The prophet Ezekiel answers that question in verse 39:2, "And I will turn thee back, and leave but the sixth part of thee" (Ezekiel 39:2 KJV).

Why will God do this? "Thus I will magnify Myself and sanctify Myself, and I will be known in the eyes of many nations. Then they shall know that I am the LORD" (Ezekiel 38:23).

Abram not only trusted God to deliver him and his men from vast armies, as do the modern armies of Israel, but he also made certain that all the glory be given to Him. God was pleased with Abram's faithfulness during this trial, for He said, "Do not be afraid, Abram. I am your shield, your exceedingly great reward" (Genesis 15:1).

The Fifth Test: The Covenant Between the Parts
God further revealed His Prophetic Blessing to Abram in a vision, ensuring him an heir who would "come from his own

body"; this heir was the son of promise. God also showed Abram that his descendants would be as countless as the stars in the heavens. Then God promised Abram and his descendants the land. Before He continued with the prophetic word, God required a sacrifice to seal the covenant. This is known as the Covenant Between the Parts (Genesis 15).

The parting of the animals had dual implication. First, it involved a sacrifice, which was commonly used in covenant making. Second, the parties that passed through the split animals bound themselves to keep the covenant or be subject to the same outcome if they violated it.

Abram must have been both overjoyed and overwhelmed to even imagine that he could father a child at his advanced age. But Abram went from excitement and hope to "horror and great darkness" (Genesis 15:12) as God revealed to him the bleak future of his descendants. "Then He said to Abram: 'Know certainly that your descendants will be strangers in a land that is not theirs, and will serve them, and they will afflict them four hundred years'" (Genesis 15:13).

Yet Abram passed the test once again and trusted God. This pleased the Lord because: "On the same day the LORD made a covenant with Abram" (Genesis 15:18). As the smoking lamp—symbolizing the presence of God—moved between the parts, God spoke the contents of the covenant to Abram: he and his descendants were to be given a Royal Land Grant that would become known as the state of Israel. The original real estate contract for the Promised Land was sealed in blood between God the Creator and Abram, the father of many nations.

The Sixth Test: Sarai and Hagar

It was not God's plan for Abram to have a son with Hagar; it was Sarai's idea. Sarai said, "See now, the LORD has restrained me from bearing children. Please, go in to my maid; perhaps I shall obtain children by her" (Genesis 16:2).

⅄ THINK ON THIS ⅄

The divine plan of God is not made of "perhaps";
His plan is certain.

Abram's test of faith came when Sarai blamed him for her barrenness, for Hagar was pregnant with his child while Sarai was not. Abram had not yet entered into the full covenant of God; he was not circumcised, therefore the child Hagar carried could not possibly be the son of covenant that God had promised him years before. Even though Abram was dismayed by the difficult decision before him, he trusted God and allowed Sarai to eventually send Hagar into the wilderness.

The Seventh Test: Circumcision

This test has to do with God's requirement for the Abrahamic covenant—the cutting away of the male foreskin. It was and still is a sign of the faith bond between God and Abraham

(Genesis 17:11). This distinguishing act symbolized another form of separation of God's seed from the world and, ultimately, from evil (Jeremiah 4:4). It is a ceremonial sign that still stands today.

This was one of Abram's most challenging and significant tests. Challenging because this act was not only unprecedented but also dangerous, for Abram was ninety-nine years of age. Significant, because circumcision was to become a required sign of the covenant between God and His people for the land of Israel from that moment on until eternity.

It was only after Abraham was circumcised and entered into the covenant that Sarah conceived the son of promise. When you think on what could have happened before this time, you fully understand what God had done to protect Abram and Sarai. Pharaoh or Abimelech could have taken Sarah and killed Abraham, but God forbade it. He made sure that Abraham and Sarah conceived and bore the son of promise just as He had declared, for no one was to intervene with the Prophetic Blessing or take the glory from the Great I AM.

Without passing this test, Abraham would have never reached his divine destiny of becoming the "father of many nations": "As for Me, behold, My covenant is with you, and you shall be a father of many nations. No longer shall your name be called Abram, but your name shall be Abraham; for I have made you a father of many nations" (Genesis 17:4–5).

❧ THINK on THIS ❧

Every time God called Abraham's name,
He prophetically called forth his divine destiny.

The Eighth Test: Hagar and Ishmael

After the birth of Isaac, Sarah became increasingly resentful of Hagar and Ishmael; they were a constant reminder of her own lack of faith in the God who had spoken the Prophetic Blessing over her and her husband years ago. "Therefore she said to Abraham, 'Cast out this bondwoman and her son; for the son of this bondwoman shall not be heir with my son, namely with Isaac'" (Genesis 21:10).

Abraham was distraught with Sarah's demand because he loved his firstborn son, Ishmael. However, the Lord said to Abraham, "Do not let it be displeasing in your sight because of the lad or because of your bondwoman. Whatever Sarah has said to you, listen to her voice; for in Isaac your seed shall be called" (Genesis 21:12). Notice that the Lord referred to Ishmael as "the lad" and the "son of the bondwoman." God was declaring that only in Isaac would His covenant be continued. Abraham put his faith in the God who never failed him and did as the Almighty had commanded; he separated himself from Hagar and sent away both her and Ishmael, the son he also loved (Genesis 21:14).

The Ninth Test: The Sacrifice

Now it came to pass after these things that God tested Abraham, and said to him, "Abraham!" And he said, "Here I am." Then He said, "Take now your son, your only son Isaac, whom you love, and go to the land of Moriah, and offer him there as a burnt offering on one of the mountains of which I shall tell you." So Abraham rose early in the morning. (Genesis 22:1–3)

Let's walk through the conversation between God and Abraham to better comprehend the absolute devotion Abraham had to God at this time in his journey to the prophetic destiny God had proclaimed over him.

How can any mortal wrap his brain around this test?

I have two sons whom I love dearly, and I cannot conceptualize such a demand. Even though Jewish scholars list this act as one of the ten trials of faith for Abraham, it is the only one that Scripture refers to as a *test*. God had intended Abraham to carry out the other nine trials to completion; however, He never planned for Abraham to sacrifice Isaac. God had promised Abraham a son to inherit the blessing; He would have never annulled His Word, for "God is not a man, that He should lie" (Numbers 23:19).

At the age of one hundred, Abraham was finally rewarded with the son of promise. What great aspirations he had for Isaac, the heir to God's Prophetic Blessing! But then God called Abraham's name—and presented him with the most difficult test.

Abraham instantly acknowledged God's voice with "Here I am," indicating that he was ready to do God's bidding. In His detailed instructions to Abraham, God told him to *offer* Isaac on the altar of sacrifice. After Abraham heard God's instruction, he could have reasoned that God had repeatedly promised him that Isaac was the link to the future destiny upon which God's promises to Abraham were based, but he had pure faith that God would prevail, so he chose to sleep instead. We can only fathom *such* peace in the time of *such* a great personal storm.

☩ THINK ON THIS ☩

When a believer is in the middle of God's will,
he has perfect peace even during the greatest crisis of his life.

Tests in Scripture are for the benefit of those being tested; for God tests none but the righteous: "The LORD tests the righteous . . . for the LORD is righteous, He loves righteousness; His countenance beholds the upright" (Psalm 11:5, 7). Daniel slept in the lions' den surrounded by impending death, and he walked out triumphantly. Jesus slept in the boat during a raging tempest that terrified His seasoned disciples who had been raised on the Sea of Galilee. This kind of perfect peace can only have one source—God.

God provided a ram as a substitute for Isaac and for Abraham's absolute submission to God's will. He then spoke the Prophetic Blessing over Abraham and Isaac once again (Genesis 22:17–18). This test ultimately established Abraham's complete devotion to God. It would lift Abraham to the pinnacle of his relationship with the Lord whom he loved so much. After Mount Moriah, Scripture never records God directly addressing Abraham again, for he had passed the ultimate test.

The Tenth Test: The Burial

This test dealt directly with the land promised in God's Prophetic Blessing. Even though the Lord had promised Abraham and his seed the entire land of Israel, when his beloved Sarah died, Abraham had to bow before the pagan inhabitants of the Promised Land and purchase a burial plot (Genesis 23).

Abraham could have demanded the land because he had already received it in covenant from God. He already owned the land. But instead, he stood firm on the purchase, which created Scripture's first documentation of a land transaction in Canaan: "So the field and the cave that is in it were deeded to Abraham by the sons of Heth as property for a burial place" (Genesis 23:20).

It is important to note that the three most explicit purchases of land in Scripture are ironically the three most contested pieces of real estate in Israel today. One is the cave of Machpelah, bought by Abraham for Sarah's burial, and located in modern-day Hebron: "And Abraham weighed out the silver for Ephron which he had named in the hearing of the sons of Heth, four hundred shekels of silver, currency of the merchants" (Genesis 23:16).

The second is Shechem, purchased by Jacob, which became the eventual site of Joseph's tomb, located in modern-day Nablus: "Then Jacob came safely to the city of Shechem, which is in the land of Canaan, when he came from Padan Aram; and he pitched his tent before the city. And he bought the parcel of land, where he had pitched his tent, from the children of Hamor, Shechem's father, for one hundred pieces of money. Then he erected an altar there and called it El Elohe Israel" (Genesis 33:18–20).

The third is the purchase of the site of the Temple, bought by David and located in Jerusalem: "Then King David said to Ornan, 'No, but I will surely buy it for the full price, for I will not take what is yours for the Lord, nor offer burnt offerings with that which costs me nothing.' So David gave Ornan six hundred shekels of gold by weight for the place. And David built there an altar to the Lord, and offered burnt offerings and peace offerings, and called on the Lord; and He answered him from heaven by fire on the altar of burnt offering" (1 Chronicles 21:24–26).

God promised the land and so much more to Abraham and his seed. He promised that Abraham's descendants would be a blessing to the world. How can this be from a people who wandered the wilderness for forty years before reaching the Promised Land? How can this be from a people who were eventually dispersed to the nations of the world? How can this be from a people who were nearly annihilated through pogroms and the Holocaust? Because God promised to take them "to a land that I will show you" (Genesis 12:1).

In Hebrew, the term *to show* refers to the land but can also mean "to make known your nature to yourself and to the world." In His infinite plan, God not only took Abraham's descendants to the land but also revealed who they were destined to become as a people.

The people whose books were burned during the pogroms now have the largest number of Nobel Prize winners on earth. The people who could not own land in Germany are now some of the world's best agronomists. The people who could not carry a gun in Nazi Poland now have one of the best military forces in the world. The Jewish people would never have *known* their nature or *shown* it to the world until they were *in* the covenant land of Israel.

✟ THINK ON THIS ✟

The God of the Bible is a God of covenant. No one reaches his or her divine destiny without walking with God in covenant. Every flower that blooms in the sacred Scripture is planted in the soil of covenant.

God made a covenant with Abraham, Isaac, and Jacob and their descendants that the land of Israel was their everlasting possession; the sign of the covenant was circumcision.

God made a covenant with Noah that He would not destroy the earth again with water; the sign of the covenant was the rainbow in the sky.

God made a covenant with King David that Israel would forever possess the land; the sign was the sun shining by day and the moon by night.

God made a blood covenant with you at the cross that the blood of Jesus Christ would cleanse you of all sin and present you faultless to the Father in heaven. The sign is the circumcision of the heart that makes you obedient to the Word of God. Everything that God does with man and for man is done in covenant.

God tested Abraham, and He will test us, for all who live godly in Christ Jesus will suffer trials and tribulations: "Beloved, do not be surprised at the fiery ordeal among you which comes upon you for your testing, as though some strange thing were happening to you . . ." (1 Peter 4:12 NASB).

ISHMAEL'S BLESSING

The Arabs of the world claim the land of Israel by virtue of the fact that Ishmael was the son of Abraham, born to Hagar. However, God made it very clear in His real estate contract that Ishmael was to be excluded as an heir to the land of Israel. The Bible records the conversation between God and Abraham as follows:

> *And Abraham said to God, "Oh, that Ishmael might live before You!" Then God said: "No, Sarah your wife shall bear you a son, and you shall call his name Isaac; I will establish My covenant with him for an everlasting covenant, and with his descendants after him. And as for Ishmael, I have heard you. Behold, I have blessed him, and will make him fruitful, and will multiply him exceedingly. He shall beget twelve princes, and I will make him a great nation. But My covenant I will establish with Isaac, whom Sarah shall bear to you at this set time next year." (Genesis 17:18–21)*

God had disconnected Ishmael from the covenant when He referred to him as "the lad" (Genesis 21:12), while calling Isaac "your only son" (Genesis 22:2). Isaac was the son of covenant born to Sarah. Abraham's name would be carried forth only through Isaac.

Likewise, the Prophetic Blessing that God spoke over Ishmael came to pass, for he was blessed greatly. His descendants of today are the OPEC nations, which control the oil-rich Persian Gulf. Isaac received the land of Israel; Ishmael received the oil of the Persian Gulf. Every time you pay for a gallon of gas, you are part of Ishmael's blessing fulfilled!

THE PROPHETIC BLESSING IS PERSONAL

Now the LORD *had said to Abram . . .*
"I will make you a great nation;
I will bless you
And make your name great;
And you shall be a blessing." (Genesis 12:1–2)

Abraham was called to a new revelation of God's will and rose to a level of faith that few have attained. God spoke to Abraham as one speaks to a friend, face-to-face. God took Abraham into His confidence, as well as into His fellowship, and made a promise of personal blessing, saying, "I will bless you . . ."

Genesis 13:2 records: "Abram was very rich in livestock, in silver, and in gold." It was a temporal earthly blessing, which was very personal.

A blessed man will experience good relationships in his marriage, with his children, and with his friends; he and his family enjoy good health and healing; he gets promoted at his place of employment. His house sells quickly while his neighbors wait for months without success. His business thrives when other businesses shrivel. All of these blessings are temporal and very personal.

Concerning a blessed man, people might say, "He has the Midas touch!" Wrong! Our power to prosper is made possible by God's faithfulness to His word through His Prophetic

Blessing. That blessing is carried over to his wife, his children, his grandchildren, and everything he puts his hand to. Wherever he goes, whatever he does succeeds. This is but a mere portion of the power of God's Prophetic Blessing upon the lives of men and nations as demonstrated by the Word of God.

The Prophetic Blessing is personal and is available to you, your children, and your grandchildren today!

SECTION 2:

THE PROPHETIC BLESSINGS

CHAPTER FIVE

TO BLESS OR NOT TO BLESS?

I will bless those who bless you,
And I will curse him who curses you;
And in you all the families of the earth shall be blessed.

—GENESIS 12:3

I have taught my congregation, America, and the nations of the world about Israel for thirty-four years. I have also authored several best-selling prophetic books on Israel and the Jewish people.[1] Presently, through Christians United for Israel (CUFI), other Christian leaders and I are endeavoring to unite America's fifty million evangelicals under one umbrella to support Israel and the Jewish people.

CUFI is currently over one million members strong and has forty-nine million Christians to go! Therefore, I would be remiss if I did not review some of the biblical history of God's eternal covenant with the Jewish people and the accounts of men and nations that have blessed or cursed the apple of God's eye.

⚜ THINK ON THIS ⚜

You cannot be anti-Semitic and receive the blessings of God.

THE ETERNAL COVENANT

Why did the apostle Paul—who affirmed he was Jewish and of the tribe of Benjamin, being named after the first king of Israel—want Gentiles to know that God had not cast off the Jewish people?

Has God cast away His people? Certainly not! . . . God has not cast away His people whom He foreknew. (Romans 11:1–2)

I say then, have they stumbled that they should fall? Certainly not! But through their fall, to provoke them to jealousy, salvation has come to the Gentiles. (Romans 11:11)

For I do not desire, brethren, that you should be ignorant of this mystery, lest you should be wise in your own opinion, that blindness in part has happened to Israel until the fullness of the Gentiles has come in. And so all Israel will be saved. (Romans 11:25–26)

REPLACEMENT THEOLOGY

St. Paul spent three chapters in the book of Romans dealing with the subject of God's relationship with the Jewish people. God *foreknew* that the nation of Israel would be put aside during this present church age. The church is guilty of following erroneous and destructive doctrines such as Replacement Theology. Replacement Theology is the teaching that the church of Jesus Christ has replaced the Jewish people in the economy of God. Replacement Theology is also called *supersessionism*, which is a particular interpretation of the New Testament that claims God's relationship with Christians supersedes His prior relationship with the Jewish people.

This destructive theology falsely presents the idea that the promises, covenants, and blessings ascribed to Israel in Scripture have been taken away from the Jews and given to the church, which has superseded them. Replacement Theology teaches that the Jewish people are subject to the curses found in the Scripture because of their rejection of Christ.

Many Christians have never heard the term *replacement theology* and are unaware that they have fallen prey to doctrinal error. These doctrines are nothing more than a form of religious anti-Semitism whose purpose is to exalt Christianity over Judaism.

⅋ THINK ON THIS ⅋

God does not make mistakes; He does not lie, and what comes from His mouth comes to pass. God does not break covenant. If God has broken covenant with the Jewish people, what confidence do we have that He will not break covenant with the Gentiles?

God is not a man, that He should lie,
Nor a son of man, that He should repent.
Has He said, and will He not do?
Or has He spoken, and will He not make it good?
(Numbers 23:19)

THE ETERNAL COVENANT

The definition of *eternal* is "to last forever, continual and always the same." The word *covenant* means to enter into "a pledge, a promise, a pact, and/or a bond." And, finally, the word *blessing* means "to consecrate, to set apart and to make holy." *God has made an eternal covenant with Israel.* It is not difficult to understand; God has set apart the Jewish people through His blessing and promise, which will not change and will last forever.

Israel has not been replaced by the church nor cast aside by the God who called Abraham to be the "father of many nations" through the Abrahamic Blessing. The Jewish people are loved of God for the *fathers' sake* (Romans 11:28).

Who are the *fathers?* Abraham, Isaac, and Jacob.

GOD'S MANDATE TO BLESS ISRAEL

I will bless those who bless you,
And I will curse him who curses you. (Genesis 12:3)

Throughout Romans 9, 10, and 11, St. Paul clearly stated that God's promise to Israel stands forever, and He will never abandon His people Israel; neither will He abandon the church.

Regarding the Jewish people, St. Paul told the Gentile Christians of Rome, "Do not boast over the branches and pride yourself at their expense. If you do boast and feel superior, remember it is not you that support the root, but the root [that supports] you" (Romans 11:18 AMP). The "root" that St. Paul was referring to is Abraham, Isaac, and Jacob.

St. Paul further instructed the Gentiles about their attitude and treatment of the Jewish people in his blockbuster declaration in Romans 15:27: "For if the Gentiles have been partakers of [the Jewish people's] spiritual things, their duty is also to minister to them in material things."

What spiritual things have the Jewish people given to Christianity? Very clearly, we owe a debt of gratitude to the Jewish people for their contributions to our faith. They have given us:

- the Word of God
- the patriarchs—Abraham, Isaac, and Jacob
- the prophets of Israel

- the first family of Christianity—Mary, Joseph, and Jesus
- the twelve disciples
- the apostle Paul

It is no wonder that Jesus said, "Salvation is of the Jews" (John 4:22). Take away the Jewish contribution to Christianity, and there would be no Christianity.

Judaism does not need Christianity to explain its existence; however, Christianity cannot explain its existence without Judaism. Without the Jewish contribution to Christianity, there would be no Savior and no salvation.[2]

Let's examine the Bible history of men and nations that have blessed the Jewish people, and learn from history that those who bless Israel will be blessed of God, but those who curse Israel will suffer the consequences of their choices.

THE TWO PHARAOHS

Consider the Pharaoh who blessed Joseph and his family by giving them the rich lands of Goshen in Egypt. These were the most fertile farmlands in the realm where a family of Jews became a great nation over the next 430 years.

Joseph, through God's revelation knowledge, saved Egypt and his own family from starvation by interpreting Pharaoh's dream. Joseph foretold the coming of seven years of abundance followed immediately by seven years of famine. This revelation changed the destiny of Egypt. To reward his wisdom, Pharaoh blessed Joseph, Joseph's family, and ultimately his own country by appointing Joseph prime minister of Egypt.

As a result of his kindness to God's chosen people, Pharaoh became the wealthiest and most powerful leader on earth. Because of the blessing of God, Egypt's highest glory was reached during the time the Jewish people dwelled there.

But there arose a pharaoh "who did not know Joseph" (Exodus 1:8). He persecuted the Jewish people. He had Jewish male babies drowned in the Nile River as a form of population control. He forced the Jews to make bricks without straw, and made their lives exceedingly grievous.

God's promise became truth: "I will curse those who curse you."

Egypt was smitten by ten plagues that destroyed their crops, killed their cattle, and turned the mighty Nile into a bloody river. Death and pestilence reeked throughout the land. When Pharaoh killed the Jewish children, God killed the firstborn of every Egyptian household that did not have the supernatural protection of the sacrificial lamb's blood over the door. As a final expression of His wrath, God drowned Pharaoh and his mighty army in the Red Sea, transforming the world's mightiest man into fish food. Exactly what Pharaoh had done to the Jewish people, God did to him and his army.

The Pharaoh who blessed the Jewish people became the richest and most powerful man on the face of the earth. The Pharaoh who tormented the Jewish people became a bloated corpse. God's Word is true! "I will bless those who bless you, and I will curse him who curses you" (Genesis 12:3).

A modern-day example of God's promise becoming truth was spoken into existence by the president of Venezuela, Hugo Chavez. He delivered the following speech at a youth rally, which was posted on YouTube for the world to see.

In his speech, Chavez was referring to the Gaza flotilla incident of May 31, 2010[3], where the Israeli Defense Force intercepted a Turkish ship carrying hundreds of pro-Palestinian activists with terrorist links and the IHH, a Turkish group, which has been labeled by the UN as a "separate hard-core group." Chavez, a fervent anti-Semite, vehemently expressed his deep hatred for Israel and the Jewish people. Listen to his self-proclaimed curse:

> Do you not see the Yankee Empire? Do you not see the Yankee Empire and the slaughter that the genocide state of Israel committed against a group of pacifists who were carrying a load of humanitarian aid?
>
> The Palestinian people in Gaza are surrounded on all sides by Israel—they don't allow them even to have water. They massacred some people . . . you saw it, correct? God forbid Alcala! If it had happened in Venezuelan waters, we would be invaded. Rest assured that we would already have been invaded!
>
> But no, since it was Israel, they are allowed to do anything. So that's an example of double moral

standards: Obama's government condemns terrorism as long as it is not personally committed by them—by the United States or its ally Israel!

They accuse us—they accuse me—of supporting terrorism. They are sponsors of terrorism!

I take this opportunity to condemn it again from the depths of my soul and my guts—the miserable state of Israel. Cursed is the state of Israel! Cursed be Israel and its terrorists and assassins, and long live the Palestinian people! And long live the Palestinian people; heroic people, and good people.

Hey, look, the Venezuelan opposition [Hugo's opposing party] has not said anything against Israel, no! Why?

Israel finances the Venezuelan opposition. They finance the counter-revolution. There are even groups of Israeli Mossad terrorists that are after me—attempting to kill me! Planning to kill me!

This is one of the threats that we have—only that we have it controlled. We know where they are within the Caribbean Islands. But we have many friends, as I have everywhere. They [Israeli Mossad] are not invisible. They are not the invisible man, and they are stupid most of the time.

Hey, they are used to fighting against defenseless people like this, like this humanitarian expedition at midnight. They dropped in from helicopters and with machine-gun fire, people who most likely were sleeping. In international waters, this is a war crime! Where is the international criminal court? Where is the United Nations? Where is the justice in this world? For the love of god, where is the justice in this world?[4]

A year later, Hugo Chavez announced he has cancer and is currently battling for his life. The populist president recently admitted that Cuban doctors had removed a baseball-sized tumor from his abdominal area.

God's Word became truth: "I will curse him who curses you."

JACOB AND THE GENTILE

The story of Jacob and Laban also confirms the Bible principle that God blesses the Gentiles through the Jewish people or judges them for their treatment of and behavior toward the apple of God's eye. Jacob went to work for his father-in-law, Laban, who was a Gentile.

Laban treated Jacob harshly by changing his wages ten times and refusing to pay Jacob what he was worth. Jacob went to his father-in-law with his resignation in hand. Knowing the blessing of God was on Jacob, Laban made an historic statement recorded in Genesis 30:27: "I have learned by experience that the LORD has blessed me [a Gentile] for your sake." And so it has been throughout history: God has blessed the Gentile people through the seed of Abraham.

A LOVER OF ISRAEL

Luke 7 tells the story of a Roman centurion—a Gentile—who had a sick servant he dearly loved. The centurion heard that a healing rabbi, Jesus of Nazareth, was coming down the road toward his house. The question was, how could this Gentile centurion, who according to the law of Moses was unclean, manage to convince a rabbi to come into his house and pray for his sick servant?

The centurion conferred with the Jewish elders, and they went out to intercept Jesus and plead the cause of the Roman centurion. The Bible record reads: "And when they [the Jewish elders] came to Jesus, they begged Him earnestly, saying that the one for whom He should do this was deserving, 'for he loves our nation, and has built us a synagogue'" (Luke 7:4–5).

Notice the reasoning the Jewish elders used with Jesus. They pleaded the cause of the centurion because he demonstrated his love for the nation of Israel by building a synagogue. The centurion's practical act of kindness toward the Jewish people was enough for Jesus to break the law of God as given to Moses, which He observed, and be willing to enter the home of the centurion to pray for his sick servant.

Miraculously, the sick servant was healed due to his master's extraordinary display of kindness to the Jewish people and faith in the healing rabbi named Jesus: "'But say the word, and my servant will be healed.' . . . And those who were sent, returning to the house, found the servant well who had been sick" (Luke 7:7, 10).

The message is very clear! When you carry out practical acts of kindness for the Jewish people, God will release His supernatural power to bless you and your household. What He did for the centurion He can do for you!

The question is: What have you done to bring practical blessings to the Jewish people and the nation of Israel?

"A GOOD REPUTATION"

I have visited Caesarea many times and find it one of the most intriguing cities in all of Israel. Caesarea, built in honor of Caesar by Herod the Great, was the center of the Roman government during the time of Christ.

Caesarea is where St. Peter went to the home of another Roman centurion named Cornelius. The Bible gives an amazing report about what happened even before Peter could finish speaking to those gathered in the house:

> While Peter was still speaking these words, the Holy Spirit fell upon all those who heard the word. And those of the circumcision who believed were astonished, as many as came with Peter, because the gift of the Holy Spirit had been poured out on the Gentiles also. For they heard them speak with tongues and magnify God. Then Peter answered, "Can anyone forbid water, that these should not be baptized who have received the Holy Spirit just as we have?" And he commanded them to be baptized in the name of the Lord. (Acts 10:44–48)

Why did God choose the house of Cornelius as the first to receive the good news of the gospel and the outpouring of the Holy Spirit? Because this Gentile was blessing the Jewish people through personal acts of kindness; so much so that he had a good reputation among the nation of the Jews. God does indeed bless those who bless Israel. "And they [the Jewish people] said, 'Cornelius the centurion [is] a just man, one who fears God and has a good reputation among all the nation of the Jews'" (Acts 10:22).

JESUS AND HIS BRETHREN

I have had the opportunity to minister all over the world for more than fifty-four years. Often I hear these words coming from overzealous Christians: "I would do anything for Jesus!" Would you really? Are you aware of Jesus' position on the Jewish people and the land of Israel? And once you become aware, are you doing anything to stand with the nation of Israel or to bless God's people? Jesus said, "He who is not with Me is against Me" (Matthew 12:30).

Jesus took a very personal position concerning God's chosen people. In Matthew 25:40, He stated, "Assuredly, I say to you, inasmuch as you did it to the least of these My brethren, you did it to Me."

Jesus called the Jewish people His "brethren." Some will try to say He was referring to the Gentile church. Not so. Before the cross of Christ, we were, as stated by St. Paul, "without Christ, being aliens from the commonwealth of

Israel and strangers from the covenants of promise, having no hope and without God in the world" (Ephesians 2:12).

Jesus was clearly talking about the Jewish people as being His brethren in Matthew 25:40. The Jewish people are "the apple of His [God's] eye" (Deuteronomy 32:10). They are the chosen people, the people of covenant, and the people whom God cherishes to this day.

In His conversation with the Samaritan woman at Jacob's well, Jesus said to her, "You [the Samaritans] worship what you do not know; we [the Jews] know what we worship, for salvation is of the Jews" (John 4:22). Simply stated, Jesus identified with the Jews during His earthly ministry.

In the last book of the Bible, Jesus is called "the Lion of the tribe of Judah" (Revelation 5:5). The word *Judah* is the name from which the word *Jew* is taken. It is important for Christians to understand that Jesus not only identified with the Jewish people in His earthly life, but He continued that relationship in Scripture after His death, burial, and resurrection—and *will indeed* continue it into eternity.

To say that you love Jesus Christ, a Jewish rabbi, while not loving your Jewish coworkers or neighbors is a contradiction in terms. It is *closet anti-Semitism.*

The Judgment of the Nations will be based on the treatment of the Jewish people: "I will also gather all nations, and bring them down to the Valley of Jehoshaphat; and I will enter into judgment with them there on account of My people, My heritage Israel" (Joel 3:2). Will you be counted as the righteous among the nations?

THE RIGHTEOUS AMONG THE NATIONS

Ask yourself this question: Do I obey God simply to receive His blessing, or do I obey God because it is the right thing to do regardless of consequences?

There was a dark time in the world's history during the twentieth century known as the Holocaust, when millions of Jews were murdered as nations remained silent. But there were individuals who heard the call of God and obeyed no matter the consequences—they are known as the Righteous Among the Nations.

Righteous Among the Nations is the term applied to non-Jews who saved Jews from Nazi persecutors without any thought of compensation or reward.[5] I will name but a few of these Gentiles to demonstrate the unconditional and selfless acts these individuals performed to save their fellow man.

- In Germany, the farmer Heinrich List sheltered a Jewish friend on his farm, and when the Nazis discovered what he had done, they arrested him and sent him to Dachau concentration camp, where he died.[6]
- Oskar Schindler saved twelve hundred Jewish factory workers from the death camps. He was arrested three times for complicity and violation of the Nuremberg Laws and had to flee to Austria to escape persecution from the Nazis. By the end of the war, Schindler was virtually destitute after using his entire fortune rescuing "Schindler's Jews" from certain death.[7]

- In the Netherlands, Joop Vesterweel, Jaap Musch, Joop Woortman, and Albertus Zefat were executed on Dutch soil for their involvement in the rescue of Jews.[8]
- In Denmark, Henry Thomsen ferried Jews across to freedom into Sweden and when arrested was sent to the Neuengamme concentration camp, where he died.[9]
- Corrie ten Boom, whom I had the pleasure of meeting, was sent to Ravensbrück concentration camp along with her father and sister after being arrested for helping many Jewish families escape from the Nazis. Both her father and beloved sister perished. The ten Boom family believed the Jews were God's chosen people; they provided kosher food for the Jewish families who stayed with them and kept the Jewish Sabbath in their honor.[10]
- In Paris, Suzanne Spaak rescued Jewish children and when discovered was executed by the Nazis on the eve of the liberation of Paris.[11]
- Adelaide Hautval did not keep silent about the Nazi cruelty and atrocities she witnessed against the Jews. Charged as a "friend of the Jews," she was deported to the Auschwitz death camp.[12]
- In Poland, the Wolski family hid several dozen Jews in an underground garden shelter on the non-Jewish side of the city. When the hiding place was discovered, the Nazis executed all of the bunker's inhabitants, including their rescuers, the Wolski family.[13]

To answer why these courageous rescuers endangered their lives through heroic acts of kindness to save the Jewish people, it is best to reflect on their responses with those of the perpetrators and the rescued when asked why they did what they did.

The Perpetrator: "I did not do it exactly as described. Besides, I was forced into it, for orders have to be obeyed. Personally, I have nothing against the Jews, and I am not responsible for my deeds."[14]

The Rescuer: "Of course I did it, and I would do it again, if called upon. I take full responsibility for my deed. I was not coaxed into it, and no one forced me to do it. Besides, it was the most natural thing."[15]

The Rescued: When Primo Levi was asked what it meant for him to be rescued by a Righteous Gentile, he answered: "However little sense there be in trying to specify why I, rather than thousands of others, managed to survive the test, I believe that it was really due to Lorenzo that I am alive today; and not so much for his material aid, as for his having constantly reminded me by his presence, by his natural and plain manner of being good, that there still existed a just world outside our own, something and someone still pure and whole, not corrupt, not savage, extraneous to hatred and terror; something difficult to define, a remote possibility of good, but for which it was worth surviving. Thanks to Lorenzo, I managed not to forget that I myself was a man."[16]

Ẏ THINK ᴏɴ THIS Ẏ

What was the result of their sacrifice? The Talmud states, "Whosoever saves one life is as though he has saved an entire world."

THE PROPHETIC CURSE

I will curse him who curses you. (Genesis 12:3)

Dietrich Bonhoeffer said, "Silence in the face of evil is itself evil; God will not hold us guiltless. Not to speak is to speak. Not to act is to act." Our generation has mastered the art of looking the other way when evil presents its face of terror and death. The prophet Obadiah clearly described the consequences of any adverse treatment of Israel:

> *For the day of the LORD upon all the nations is near;*
> *As you have done, it shall be done to you;*
> *Your reprisal shall return upon your own head.*
> *For as you drank on My holy mountain,*
> *So shall all the nations drink continually;*
> *Yes, they shall drink, and swallow,*
> *And they shall be as though they had never been.*
> *(Obadiah 1:15–16)*

Few modern-day Christians are aware of the horror inflicted upon the Jewish people over the centuries immediately following the crucifixion of Christ. I have detailed much of this atrocious history in my book *In Defense of Israel*; however, I will capsulize a few recorded historical incidences.[17]

In AD 70, four decades after the crucifixion of Jesus, the Roman army, under the leadership of Titus, surrounded the city of Jerusalem, allowing no one to enter or leave. The historian Josephus chronicled the horrible conditions, stating that there was such severe starvation that one million Jewish people died.

After the siege of Jerusalem, seventy thousand Jewish men were taken as slaves to Italy to build the Roman coliseum where Christians would later be martyred. This was the beginning of what history calls the *Diaspora*—the scattering of the Jewish people throughout the nations of the world.

Then came the rabid anti-Semite John Chrysostom, leader of the Roman church during the fourth century. Chrysostom authored eight homilies that incited hatred toward the Jews by labeling them "the Christ killers." This brand has followed the Jews ever since. In fact, I have heard with my own ears people still referring to the Jewish people by this malicious and slanderous title.

There were nine campaigns known as the Crusades that spanned the years 1096 through 1272. The Crusaders, on their way through Europe to liberate the Holy Land from the "infidels," massacred entire Jewish communities numbering in the tens of thousands. The first Crusaders to enter Jerusalem rounded up more than nine hundred men, women, and children in the local synagogue, set it on fire, and marched around the synagogue singing "Christ, We Adore Thee" as the Jews in the synagogue were burned alive.[18]

The first Tribunal, commonly referred to as the Spanish Inquisition, was held in 1480, and thousands of Jews were burned alive at the stake by those who carried the sign of the cross on their lances. Manuals were printed to assist the Spanish in identifying Jewish families in order to drive them out of Spain. King Ferdinand and Queen Isabella had issued the Edict of Expulsion in 1492, which declared that on a certain day all the Jews of Spain were to be expelled or killed. To avoid genocide, desperate Jewish parents gave up their children to Christian families who promised to raise them as their own.

The golden age of Spain came to an end because God had made a prophetic promise: "I will curse those who curse you." Today Spain has been invaded by a tidal wave of radical Islam committed to Spain's destruction. The Jerusalem Center of Public Affairs recently published this quote from al-Qaeda: "Al-Qaeda: The Next Goal Is to Liberate Spain from the Infidels."[19]

A similar historical outcome has occurred in the British Empire. Derek Prince—who was not only my friend but my mentor—walked me through Scripture and historical accounts of the judgments of God on the nations or the individuals that cursed the Jewish people:

Britain emerged victorious from two World Wars, retaining intact an empire that was perhaps the most extensive in human history. It was said at the time, "the sun never sets on the British Empire."

But in 1947–48, as the British mandate gave the British power over what was then called Palestine, Britain opposed and attempted to thwart the rebirth of Israel as a sovereign nation with her own state. Since I was living in Jerusalem throughout this period I make this statement as an eye-witness of what actually took place.

From that very moment in history, Britain's empire underwent a process of decline and disintegration so rapid and total that it cannot be accounted for by the relevant political, military or economic factors. Today, less than a generation later, Britain—like Spain—is a struggling, second-rate power.[20]

The prophet Isaiah wrote, "For the nation and kingdom which will not serve you [Israel] shall perish, and those nations shall be utterly ruined" (Isaiah 60:12).

The pages of world history bear witness to this fact: every nation or empire that has persecuted or tried to destroy the Jewish people or attempted to take the land of Israel has been cursed by God Almighty.

What is left of these nations? Where is Pharaoh and his mighty army? Where are the Babylonians? Where are the Assyrians? Where is the Ottoman Empire? Where is that lunatic Adolf Hitler and his goose-stepping Nazi hordes? They are as though they had never been—buried in the boneyard of human history![21]

Then . . .	Now . . .
Egyptian Empire . . . *gone*	Egypt—ruled by the Islamic Brotherhood
Philistines . . . *gone*	Gaza—Under Hamas control (Islamic Resistance Movement)
Assyrian Empire . . . *gone*	Nonexistent—"as though they had never been" (Obadiah 1:16)
Babylonian Empire . . . *gone*	Iraq—Under the control of four warring political parties: 1. Secular nationalist parties 2. Shi'a Muslim parties 3. Sunni Muslim parties 4. Kurdish parties
Persian Empire . . . *gone*	Iran—Ruled by the Ayatollah Khomeini and President Mahmoud Ahmadinejad, who has sworn to "wipe Israel off the map." "They have said, 'Come, and let us cut them off from being a nation, that the name of Israel may be remembered no more'" (Psalm 83:4).
Greek Empire . . . *gone*	Greece—Ready to declare national bankruptcy[22]
Roman Empire . . . *gone*	Nonexistent
Byzantine Empire . . . *gone*	Nonexistent
Spanish Empire . . . *gone*	Spain—Being overtaken by radical Islam[23]
Nazi Germany . . . *gone*	Neo-Nazism on the rise[24]

Where are Israel and the Jewish people? They are alive and well, thriving and prospering in their covenant land just as God promised Abraham, Isaac, and Jacob in His Prophetic Blessing, written and recorded for all eternity in the book of Genesis.

Where does America stand as a nation in regard to Israel? Are we blessing or cursing the apple of God's eye? Will America's name be added to the list of cursed nations? We must, as Bible-believing Americans, never allow any group, political party, or administration to lead our nation on a path of certain destruction! Either we stand with Israel, or we, too, shall suffer the same fate as those who stood against Israel.

ISRAEL SHALL BLESS

And you shall be a blessing. . . .
And in you all the families of the earth shall be blessed.
(Genesis 12:2–3)

In the first chapter, I cited astounding statistics regarding the accomplishments of the Jewish people, who only represent .0021 percent of the total population of the world. It bears repeating! These achievements are documented proof that God's prophetic blessings and covenants are never void.

In the book *The Golden Age of Jewish Achievement*, Steven Pease compiled an exhaustive catalog of the Jewish contributions to mankind. Just skimming through the table of contents will give you a sense of awe. How can so few do so much in every area of accomplishment known to man: in science, inventions, education, economics, politics, sports, performing arts, radio and television, business . . . ? The categories go on and on!

If I were to choose just the field of science and record the numerous medical breakthroughs that have saved millions upon millions of lives, that alone fulfills the prophetic scripture: "And in you all families of the earth shall be blessed."

God cataloged His own list of achievements by His chosen people, centuries before they happened! You will find them in Deuteronomy 28:2–6, which begins with, "And all these blessings shall come upon you and overtake you, because you obey the voice of the LORD your God":

1. *"Blessed shall you be in the city"*—Forbes 400 named the world's top twenty-five Real Estate Developers: eighteen of the twenty-five are Jewish.[25]
2. *"Blessed shall you be in the country"*—Despite over half of its land area being desert, Israel produces 95 percent of its country's food needs.[26]
3. *"Blessed shall be the fruit of your body"*—One-quarter of the world's Nobel Prize recipients have been Jewish.[27]
4. *"The produce of your ground and the increase of your herds, the increase of your cattle and the offspring of your flocks"*—Israel's cows, a high-yielding,

TO BLESS OR NOT TO BLESS?

disease-resistant breed, produce the most milk in the world.[28]

5. *"Blessed shall be your basket and your kneading bowl"*— Israel grows its own grains, fruits, and vegetables in a country the size of Rhode Island.[29]

6. *"Blessed shall you be when you come in, and blessed shall you be when you go out"*—God blessed Abraham's seed when they entered the land, and He will continue to do so until Messiah returns.

PRAY FOR THE PEACE OF JERUSALEM

In Psalm 122:6–7, King David commanded all believers, "Pray for the peace of Jerusalem: 'May they prosper who love you. Peace be within your walls, prosperity within your palaces.'"

Look at the blessings that come to the Christian who honors this command to pray for the peace of Jerusalem. Here again the Word of God thunders, "May they prosper who love you." That prosperity is a *personal* prosperity, just as Abraham received. Again, allow me to quote my dear friend Derek Prince, who was a lover and defender of Israel:

A challenging, scriptural pattern of this kind of praying is provided by Daniel, who set himself to pray three times daily with his window open toward Jerusalem. Daniel's prayers so disturbed Satan and threatened his kingdom that he used the jealousy of evil men to bring about a change in the laws of the entire

Persian Empire that would make Daniel's prayers illegal. On the other hand, praying for Jerusalem meant so much to Daniel that he preferred to be cast into the lions' den rather than give up his praying for the peace of Jerusalem.[30]

The power of the Prophetic Blessing concludes with "Peace be within your walls, prosperity within your palaces."

This is the scriptural pathway to prosperity—not merely in a financial or material sense, but an abiding assurance of God's favor, provision, and protection. It is a matter of historical record that if Jerusalem is at peace, the world is at peace. If Jerusalem is at war, then the world is at war.

As I write these words, the winds of war are blowing over the Middle East. If Iran is allowed to become a nuclear nation, Israel will be at war, and that war will engulf the earth. The point is, when you pray for the peace of Jerusalem, you are praying for peace in America, in Europe, in Canada, or in whatever nation you live.

⅋ THINK on THIS ⅋

World peace begins with peace in Jerusalem. That's not my opinion; it's God's: "For Zion's [Israel's] sake I will not hold My peace, and for Jerusalem's sake I will not rest" (Isaiah 62:1).

MY CALL TO BLESS

Diana and I went to Israel for the first time in the spring of 1978, not knowing that this journey would change our lives and the lives of our children and grandchildren forever! As I walked the cobblestone streets of Jerusalem, I felt a very special presence there—a presence I have never felt anywhere else.

Jerusalem is the most unique city in the world. The psalmist called it "the city of God" (Psalm 87:3). This is where Abraham took Isaac to the mount to offer him to God; this is the city where Jeremiah and Isaiah scripted principles of righteousness that would become the moral compass for Western civilization.

Jerusalem is where Jesus Christ carried His cross to Calvary to die for the sins of the world. This is the city from which Jesus Christ will rule the world in an eternal kingdom with a rod of iron, and that kingdom will never end. It is the city where kings, queens, prime ministers, and presidents will stand in line to bow at the feet of Jesus Christ, for "every knee should bow . . . every tongue should confess that Jesus Christ is Lord, to the glory of God the Father" (Philippians 2:10–11).

As I walked in the footsteps of Jesus, I made my way to the Western Wall and began doing what has become the highlight of my thirty trips to Israel—praying to the God of Abraham, Isaac, and Jacob on holy ground where a rabbi, Jesus of Nazareth, once walked with His twelve disciples.

As I prayed, I looked over my left shoulder and saw an elderly Jewish man sitting down, draped in his prayer shawl, praying earnestly, rocking back and forth as he read and kissed the Torah. As I watched him, I felt the Lord say to me, *That man is your spiritual brother, and you know nothing about him. He is terrified of you. I want you to do everything in your power to bring Christians and Jews together in an atmosphere of love and mutual respect for the rest of your life.*

I was stunned!

Sometimes, when you start talking to God, He says things to you that are not on your agenda. I pulled my prayer list out of my pocket to refocus on my *real reason* for being there. I wasn't ready for my well-ordered life to be turned upside down by a divine commission from heaven.

As I attempted to pray through my list, the thought kept crossing my mind that continuing to pray about the known will of God was in fact rebellion against God. Jesus said, "You are My friends if you do whatever I command you" (John 15:14).

Walking away from the Western Wall, I started looking for Diana, who was praying at the women's section of the Wall. I thought for a moment, *Should I tell her what had just happened or wait until later?* Diana is the love of my life, my soul partner; I can't keep anything from her. She knows me too well. I saw her coming toward me with that bright, radiant smile on her Latin face and thought, *She's happy, so I might as well tell her now.*

I recounted my experience, and she looked at me incredulously and asked, "However are you going to do that? Christians and Jews have been fighting each other for two thousand years, and you think you can stop that?"

I could feel the hair on the back of my neck start to rise, and I thunderously responded, "I don't think I'm supposed to stop anything. I do believe that the Lord just *called me* to start reaching out to the Jewish community and expressing our debt of gratitude for their contributions to Christianity and the world. I don't know how to get started; I don't personally know one rabbi in our city, and I don't know anyone anywhere doing anything that's pro-Israel! I only know I'm supposed to try!"

Diana responded, "Oh, okay. Well, let's go shopping!" My wife loves to shop; she shops as though she's on a mission from God to save the world. Minutes later we found ourselves in a Judaic antiquities store called the Harp of David. I saw a prayer shawl like the one draped over the man praying at the Wall. I bought it and later realized that it had been designed by God Himself (Numbers 15:37–41)!

As Diana was filling her basket as if she were gathering fragments from the miracle of the loaves and fishes, I turned the corner and to my delight was face-to-face with my obsession—books! I'm a book fanatic! I can spend hours in a bookstore. I have a library filled with over five thousand volumes, most of which I've read, thirty-two of which I have written.

Within minutes I had purchased several books dealing

with the history of Israel, the Crusades, and the Spanish Inquisition. I saw books on the shelf that I had never seen before—books about the harvest of hatred that produced the Holocaust, the rebirth of Israel in 1948, and the ingathering of the exiles from around the world to fulfill the words of the Old Testament prophets. I bought all that Diana and I could carry.

We returned to our home in San Antonio, and I began to consume their contents. At this point in my life, I had seminary training and two liberal arts degrees from outstanding universities, yet I discovered I knew absolutely nothing about the Jewish people that was written after Paul's epistles.

I was shocked to discover that in his later years, Martin Luther wrote one of the most anti-Semitic documents in history, called "Concerning the Jews and Their Lies." Its content was so vile and vicious I became depressed. How could the man who started the Reformation be such a vile anti-Semite? I put the book down and wanted to burn it. In his day, Hitler had reprinted Luther's book and used it as propaganda against the Jews in his Third Reich, which was the flame that ignited the gas chambers.

Over the next three years, I consumed every volume of credible literature on the Jewish people and the history of the land of Israel. I began to piece together incidents in my childhood, like the day in 1948 that my father sat in our small kitchen glued to the radio listening to the news declaring the statehood of Israel. I remember my father telling our family that Israel's rebirth fulfilled the prophecy of Isaiah 66:8: "Who has heard such a thing? Who has seen such things? Shall the earth be made to give birth in one day? Or shall a nation be born at once? For as soon as Zion was in labor, she gave birth to her children."

I began to teach the membership of Cornerstone Church the Bible's reasons why every Christian should stand up and speak up for Israel and the Jewish people (Isaiah 62:1). I studied the mysteries of the prayer shawl, and my congregation was amazed as I taught them that it was overflowing with spiritual meaning for Christians (Numbers 15:37–41).

Thirty-six months had passed. I had educated myself on a topic about which there was and still remains global ignorance regarding Israel and the sinister force of anti-Semitism that flows like an underground poisoned stream—unseen and undetected. Every few decades this toxic stream swells into a river of death and destruction.

But I still didn't know what to do with the wealth of information I had consumed.

Then it happened!

On June 7, 1981, I sat down to listen to the evening news and discovered that during a surprise air strike called "Operation Babylon" the Israeli Defense Forces destroyed the nuclear reactor in Iraq, thereby removing this deadly force from the hands of a mad man—Saddam Hussein. It was wonderful!

"Diana, come listen to this!"

"What happened?" she asked.

"God bless the IDF and Prime Minister Menachem Begin. Israel has blasted the nuclear power plant at Osiris off the face of the earth!"

We listened and discovered that the liberal media was less than pleased with Israel. For the next few days, the gurus of *"It's Israel's Fault"* went after Israel tooth and claw. I felt that Israel and the Jewish people should be congratulated, not condemned.

Then it hit me!

"Diana, this is what we've been waiting for! We are going to have a citywide event called 'The Night to Honor Israel'! We'll invite all the pastors of the city. We'll take our choir, our orchestra, our television cameras and show America this celebration honoring Israel."

As I grabbed my yellow legal pad and started writing down all my ideas, Diana calmly said, "Don't you think you should ask the Jewish community if they want to do this?"

"That's a good idea!" I calmed down and begin to think. "Who would I contact?" I soon found out about the Jewish Federation where all things kosher must be approved and placed on the sacred pages of the community calendar.

I went to the Federation the next day and told the executive director that I wanted to conduct a citywide "Night to Honor Israel." He looked at me as if I had a contagious rash. Then it dawned on me—*This is not going to be easy. I don't believe God sent them the same memo He sent me!*

The Jewish people, when confronted with something new, start having a series of passionate committee meetings. For the first time, I experienced the meaning of the saying "Where you have two Jews, you have three opinions."

After several lively committee meetings, Rabbi Arnold Scheinberg of Rodfei Shalom Synagogue put his name and reputation on the line by suggesting, "Maybe this man is a friend." That night the Jewish community in San Antonio crossed a bridge that changed the course of history.

As soon as Rabbi Scheinberg and I appeared in the local newspaper announcing the event, death threats began pouring in. Soon after, the windows of my car were shot out in front of our home. Nonetheless, on September 10, 1981, God breathed life into the first "Night to Honor Israel." Little did we know thirty-one years ago that, through Christians United for Israel (CUFI), we would be hosting more than forty-five pro-Israel events every month throughout America.[31] If you are not a member of CUFI, I encourage you to join today by going online to www.CUFI.org.

Taking our lead from St. Paul in Romans 15:27, John Hagee Ministries has, through the gifts of generous partners, donated more than $70 million to humanitarian causes throughout Israel.

✠ THINK on THIS ✠

The blessing is personal! God mandates us to bless the
Jewish people and promises personal blessings to those
who obey Him.

I will never forget the Sunday when Dr. W. A. Criswell visited Cornerstone Church and spoke the Prophetic Blessing over Diana and me. What would bring the senior pastor of the First Baptist Church of Dallas, a giant among evangelical Christians for more than fifty years, together with a charismatic? Israel!

Diana and I knelt before this godly man as he laid hands on our heads and declared, "I know by experience that the blessings that have followed me all the days of my life are a result of blessing Israel, and I know that the blessings that will come to you and to your seed will be because of your love for the Jewish people." How true!

I can say without a doubt that the Lord has stayed true to the Abrahamic Blessing, for He has richly blessed my life and the lives of my family members. We have been blessed in our health, we have prospered above and beyond what we thought possible, our ministry has flourished, we have priceless relationships—the favor of God has overtaken us! We have not been without afflictions, but God Almighty has delivered us from them all.

We heard *the call*; we have obeyed His mandate, and God has been faithful to do what He said He would do.

There is no secret to receiving the blessing of the Lord above and beyond what you are able to ask or imagine. The key is finding out what God wants done—and doing it! God's clear message, beginning in Genesis 12 and continuing through the closing pages of Revelation, is to bless Israel and watch the power of the Prophetic Blessing explode in your life.

What is the secret to the numerical and spiritual growth and global gospel outreach of Cornerstone Church? There are not enough pages left in this book to recount the blessings that God has poured out upon our congregation. We have been blessed for our willing obedience to the Word of God in blessing the Jewish people and Israel. I invite the skeptics to try it; stand back and watch the blessings of God explode in your personal, professional, and spiritual life!

⅋ THINK ON THIS ⅋

God's blessings are not measured by what we do—
they are measured by who He is!

Chapter Six

THE BLESSINGS FULFILLED

All these are the twelve tribes of Israel, and this is what their father spoke to them. And he blessed them; he blessed each one according to his own blessing.

—Genesis 49:28

Joseph walks up the massive marble steps leading into the lavish palace he calls home. As the reigning monarch in Egypt, second only to Pharaoh, Joseph has the power of life and death, but today he will humbly bow before his aged father, Jacob, to receive the Prophetic Blessing.

Joseph holds the hands of his two Egyptian-born sons, Ephraim and Manasseh. Slaves respectfully open the towering palace doors, allowing the three to enter into the long corridor filled with polished stone images of Egypt's powerless gods. Joseph and his sons walk into the palatial chamber adorned with royal blue fabric clasped by chains of gold.

In the center of the room sits God's appointed messenger of the Prophetic Blessing, a man whose words are about to shape the future of Israel—Jacob the patriarch. Joseph's cherished father is living his final moments as he imparts the Prophetic Blessings over his two grandsons and his twelve sons. Each would appear before him with fear and trembling, because his words, inspired by the Holy Spirit, would shape each man's future.

It is the judgment seat of Jacob.

THE PROPHETIC BLESSING GIVEN TO EPHRAIM AND MANASSEH

Then Israel saw Joseph's sons, and said, "Who are these?" And Joseph said to his father, "They are my sons, whom God has given me in this place." And he said, "Please bring them to me, and I will bless them." (Genesis 48:8–9)

The Prophetic Blessing of Ephraim and Manasseh, given by their grandfather Jacob, is one of the most sacred blessings in Scripture.

Ephraim and Manasseh were over seventeen years of age, and had been born before Jacob came to Egypt. They were to become two separate tribes of Israel—a double blessing for their father, Joseph, who had saved the civilized world from starvation with his gift of revelation about Egypt's seven good years and the seven years of famine.

Even though Ephram and Manasseh would become tribes, Israel, as a nation, would continue to have only twelve tribes because the tribe of Levi "owned no land" and from generation to generation served the nation of Israel as priests regarding spirtual matters. The purpose of the tribe of Levi is further explained by Moses in Numbers chapter 3.

The tribe of Levi was set apart by God Himself to perform holy service in the tabernacle of wilderness and in the Temple (Numbers 18). Why did God set them apart? He answered that question in Numbers 3:11–13:

Then the Lord spoke to Moses, saying: "Now behold, I Myself have taken the Levites from among the children of Israel instead of every firstborn who opens the womb among the children of Israel. Therefore the Levites shall be Mine, because all the firstborn are Mine. On the day that I struck all the firstborn in the land of Egypt, I sanctified to Myself all the firstborn in Israel, both man and beast. They shall be Mine: I am the Lord.

The Prophetic Blessing that Jacob declares over his twelve sons explains that Levi's descendants were to be scattered across Israel and not counted as a tribe. The Levites would become high priests who were not given any land.

Jacob asks Joseph, "Who are these?" referring to Joseph's two sons. We know from Scripture that Jacob's eyesight was dim from old age (Genesis 48:10), yet in the next verse he clearly states, "God has also shown me your offspring!" Jacob is revealing that although his natural eyesight is too dim to see his two grandsons, the Holy Spirit has given him the revelation of their future for centuries to come.

What Jacob does when his grandsons stand before him is a generational model for every father and grandfather who desires to pass on the power of the blessing to the next generation: "[Jacob] kissed them and embraced them" (Genesis 48:10).

Prior to this, an elderly grandfather (Jacob) told one of the most powerful men on the earth, his son Joseph, to "bring them and I will bless them." This is a perfect demonstration of spiritual authority in practice by three generations. Sadly, there has been a complete breakdown of spiritual authority in the American home. I have discovered in my global travels that the farther from America I get, the more respectful the children become.

So I have this question for every father reading this book: How often do you kiss and hug your children or grandchildren?

When my five children lived at home with us, it was something I did every day. One particular day my oldest son, Christopher, who was in middle school at the time, slipped out of the house without his good-morning hug and kiss.

I got in my car and drove one block to where he was

waiting for the school bus with about ten of his friends. I stopped the car, got out, and walked toward Chris.

My father never hugged or kissed me; it was simply not the manly thing to do. However, my mother could hug you and lift you into another world. My hugging instincts come from her.

Chris saw me get out of the car, and he knew what was about to happen. He dropped his books and started running down the street screaming, "No! No! No!" I knew he didn't want a public display of affection in front of his school friends, but I chased him nonetheless.

As he ran down the sidewalk screaming, a woman came out of her house wearing a bathrobe and enough scrap-iron rollers in her hair to make a boat anchor. She stood on her porch, pointed her bony finger at me, and screamed, "Stop or I'll call the police!" I shouted back in a firm and clear voice, "Lady, I am only trying to kiss my son good-bye!"

In those days, I could outrun Chris in my Sunday suit. I caught him, hugged and kissed him, returned to my car, and drove off as the cheers from his friends erupted.

It was a great day!

Jacob, the patriarch, hugged and kissed his own . . . shouldn't we?

Jacob prepares to impart the supernatural Prophetic Blessing on Manasseh and Ephraim—the next generation. Remember, it is the birthright of the firstborn to receive the greater blessing.

By tradition, Jacob was to place his right hand upon the firstborn because the right hand in the Bible is the position of power. Jesus stands at the right hand of God, the position of power and prominence (Acts 7:55). As Jesus described the sheep and goat nations in Matthew 25, the sheep are on the right hand and the goats are on the left (v. 33).

Scripture describes the blessing Jacob gave to Ephraim and Manasseh with exact detail, as God was establishing a divine principle that would be carried out at the cross of Christ. It is the mystery of the blessing of the crossed hands.

> *And Joseph took them both, Ephraim with his right hand toward Israel's [Jacob's] left hand, and Manasseh with his left hand towards Israel's right hand, and brought them near him. (Genesis 48:13)*

Picture the scene in the theater of your mind. Joseph is bringing the firstborn, Manasseh, to Jacob's right hand—the hand of power and superior blessing. He is bringing Ephraim, the second born, to Jacob's left hand, as the custom was that the second born receive the lesser blessing.

But then Jacob shocks Joseph by crossing his hands over the heads of Manasseh and Ephraim. Jacob puts his right hand on Ephraim, the second born, and his left hand on Manasseh, the firstborn. The historic drama is captured in Genesis 48:17–19:

Now when Joseph saw that his father laid his right hand on the head of Ephraim, it displeased him; so he took hold of his father's hand to remove it from Ephraim's head to Manasseh's head. And Joseph said to his father, "Not so, my father, for this one is the firstborn; put your right hand on his head." But his father refused and said, "I know, my son, I know. He also shall become a people, and he also shall be great; but truly his younger brother shall be greater than he, and his descendants shall become a multitude of nations."

JACOB'S PROPHETIC BLESSING FULFILLED

As was the Holy Spirit's intention, Ephraim, the younger, received the right hand of blessing, which was the greater blessing. Ephraim became the leader over Manasseh. Later in the history of Israel they both marched under the banner of Ephraim through the wilderness, as described in the book of Numbers.

The tribe of Ephraim produced a series of great leaders, including Joshua, who led Israel when Moses died. The right hand of blessing changed the course of history for Israel as well as directing the lives of Manasseh and Ephraim. God is sovereign; He is not bound by the customs or traditions of men. Consider the ministerial heritage of the Hagee family through the second son.

The original John Hagee, who came to America from

Germany before the Constitution of the United States was signed, was a Moravian seeking religious freedom. Since the original Hagees' arrival in America, forty-eight descendants of the family have preached the gospel all the days of their adult life. I am number forty-seven, and my son Matthew is the forty-eighth.

In relationship to the blessing of the crossed hands, for more than one hundred years in our family it has been the second son of the second son who served in the ministry. My grandfather, John Christopher Hagee, was the second son born to a second son. My father, William Bythel Hagee, was the second son of John Christopher Hagee. I, John Charles Hagee, am the second son of William Bythel Hagee. Matthew Charles Hagee is my second-born son, and he has two sons, John William and Joel Charles. Will the future be shaped by the past?

JACOB'S TWELVE SONS

And Jacob called his sons and said, "Gather together, that I may tell you what shall befall you in the last days." (Genesis 49:1)

Jacob, the man who wrestled with God, knows he is living his last days. He calls his twelve sons to his bedside to impart the Prophetic Blessing over each one of them. Genesis 49 is perhaps one of the most overlooked portions of Scripture.

Its writings paint a stunning prophetic masterpiece of the future of Israel: of her people, of Christ's redemption, and of His return.

Jacob is sitting on the edge of his bed, his feet planted on the floor as he leans on his walking stick (Hebrews 11:21). Jacob's twelve sons are in the room. Their faces are somber, for they know their father, a spiritual giant who formed the threefold cord of Abraham, Isaac, and Jacob, is about to speak forth their future as the twelve tribes of Israel.

Jacob lifts his aged hand and motions his sons to gather close: "Gather together, that I may tell you what shall befall you in *the last days*" (Genesis 49:1).

The phrase *the last days* is an eschatological expression referring to the "time of the end" (Daniel 12:4, 9). The words that Jacob speaks under the anointing of the Holy Spirit will mold the future of Israel until Messiah comes again.

The sons surround Jacob as the patriarch's piercing eyes penetrate behind the veil of each of their lives to reveal the hidden things . . . things for which they would be commended or chastised. It is indeed the judgment seat of Jacob.

This scene is a type and shadow of the judgment seat of Christ where, according to the apostle Paul, "We must all appear . . . that each one may receive the things done in the body, according to what he has done, whether good or bad" (2 Corinthians 5:10). We will all stand before Jesus Christ just as Jacob's twelve sons stood before him. We too will face a final judgment that will determine our reward in heaven.

Let's take a closer look at one of the most significant spiritual events in Scripture. Listen to Jacob speak the Prophetic Blessing over his twelve sons:

Reuben

Reuben, you are my firstborn,
My might and the beginning of my strength,
The excellency of dignity and the excellency of power.
(Genesis 49:3)

As Reuben hears his father's first words, the anxious and worried expression melts from his face; a new confidence fills his heart and soul. Reuben squares his shoulders, his face radiant with anticipation. He was Jacob and Leah's first son, surely he would receive the greater blessing!

Reuben's thoughts race: *I'm going to get the double portion; I'm going to get more than my brothers. My seed and I are going to be the leaders of the family for generations to come!*

Jacob continues to speak. "My might and the beginning of my strength, the excellency of dignity and the excellency of power" (Genesis 49:3).

Reuben's spirit is soaring on celestial wings! *That must mean I'm going to get the priesthood; the land will be named after me.* However, the ensuing words that come from Jacob's mouth cut Reuben like a two-edged sword.

Reuben's spirit comes crashing back to earth as he is overcome by one declarative sentence pronounced by his father . . . "Unstable as water, you shall not excel" (Genesis 49:4).

Everyone in the room gasps; Reuben's face turns ashen: *Unstable? Like water?* His thoughts are spinning, causing him to nearly swoon. Water always takes the path of least resistance, a trait that makes men and rivers crooked. The Holy Spirit of the Living God who now speaks through Jacob knows that Reuben lacks character, courage, and conviction to be a leader among the tribes.

"You shall not excel!" These words echo in Reuben's mind, and his euphoria vanishes like mist driven by the hot wind. God and the Holy Spirit X-rayed Reuben's soul—Jacob merely read the X-ray. This prophetic proclamation will ordain Reuben's future and the future of his family until Messiah comes again.

The Prophetic Blessing Fulfilled

Reuben excelled in nothing—his tribe never rose to prominence in Israel. Not one of the judges was a Reubenite. Reuben was the first tribe to demand their inheritance and, careless of consequences, rashly chose the wrong side of the Jordan. Reuben was the first tribe to be carried into captivity by the Assyrians (1 Chronicles 5:26).[1]

Yet the worst is still to come for Reuben. Even though Jacob's eyesight is feeble, his stare pierces Reuben as his words present a scathing declaration over his firstborn's unconfessed sexual sin: "Because you went up to your father's bed; then you defiled it—he went up to my couch" (Genesis 49:4).

Forty years earlier, Reuben went to the bed of his father, Jacob, and had sex with Jacob's concubine Bilhah. There had been ample time to confess this grievous sin and receive forgiveness; instead Reuben chose to cover up his adulterous act behind the pretense that the sin never occurred.

On this day of days, when all things hidden are being exposed, Reuben reaps what his life has sown. This prophetic proclamation over Reuben is historical proof that unconfessed sins will find us out, and all our hopes of what we might have been in the eternal kingdom will be shattered: broken "with a rod of iron" and dashed "like a potter's vessel" (Psalm 2:9). If there is hidden sin in your life, *confess it now*. Our loving Father God is eager to forgive, for "if we confess our sins, He is faithful and just to forgive us our sins" (1 John 1:9).

Reuben shuffles to the back of the room, his shoulders stooped, his father's words still ringing in his ears: *"You shall not excel!"*

Simeon and Levi

The brothers Simeon and Levi step forward to the judgment seat of Jacob. It is their time to give account for the deeds done in their lifetimes. Because of Reuben's verbal chastisement, Simeon and Levi now know that this day of Prophetic Blessing has become a day of reckoning.

The two brothers, sons of Leah, stand before the patriarch, who speaks:

Simeon and Levi are brothers;
Instruments of cruelty are in their dwelling place. (Genesis 49:5)

The two brothers, Leah's second and third sons, glance at each other and remember their sister Dinah, who had been raped by Shechem. Shechem loved Dinah and asked his father, Hamor, to request her hand in marriage. Hamor's family offered a dowry, friendship, and a proposal that the two peoples live in peace together. However, the sons of Jacob refused, saying:

We cannot do this thing, to give our sister to one who is uncircumcised, for that would be a reproach to us. But on this condition we will consent to you: If you will become as we are, if every male of you is circumcised, then we will give our daughters to you, and we will take your daughters to us; and we will dwell with you, and we will become one people. But if you will not heed us and be circumcised, then we will take our daughter and be gone. (Genesis 34:14–17)

This was pure deception, for Simeon and Levi had no intention of giving Dinah to Shechem or of living in peace with the native people. Instead, the brothers plotted to kill them.

The male citizens of Shechem agreed to be circumcised to show their sincerity in the covenant of marriage between Dinah and Shechem.

Three days after the circumcision, when the men of Shechem were in great pain, Simeon and Levi took their swords and killed every male in the city. They killed Shechem and his father, took Dinah from his house, and left (Genesis 34:25–26).

They stole the flocks and herds and donkeys and carried off all their wealth and all the women and children, taking as plunder everything in the houses (Genesis 34:28–29).

It was enough to make *The Godfather* look like *The Brady Bunch*—mass slaughter and grand theft on an unthinkable scale—and the two leaders of the pack were Simeon and Levi.

Jacob looks at the two sons of Leah and considers them as one: "Simeon and Levi are brothers" (Genesis 49:5). The brothers glance at each other wondering how Jacob would judge them for Shechem these many years later. They didn't have to wait long.

Jacob's next words speak of their criminal behavior: "Instruments of cruelty. . . .

For in their anger they slew a man,
And in their self-will they hamstrung an ox" (Genesis 49:5–6).

Their sin—like Reuben's—was one of weakness: their unbridled rage produced premeditated mass murder. Jacob's prophetic statement continues: "Cursed be their anger, for it is fierce; and their wrath, for it is cruel! I will divide them in Jacob and scatter them in Israel" (Genesis 49:7).

The Prophetic Blessing Fulfilled

Simeon's inheritance for the land was included in the share of the tribe of Judah (Joshua 19:9). His tribe would eventually be dispersed throughout Israel among the tribes of Ephraim, Manasseh, and Naphtali (2 Chronicles 34:6). Even Moses passed over Simeon: "When Moses came to bless the tribes, he transformed Jacob's judgment of Levi into a blessing, but Simeon he passed over in silence"[2] (Deuteronomy 33:8–11).

However, in Levi we see the grace of God in action. God scattered Levi and his descendants throughout Israel, just as He did Simeon's. Levi was judiciously scattered among the people, but because of a bold stand for God while in the wilderness (Exodus 32:26), God made him the high priest over the nation of Israel.

This action would become a blessing, for the Levites would eventually inhabit most of the kingdom of Israel.[3] Think of it: only the grace of God could take a cruel man like Levi and make him the head of all the priests in Israel. God's Prophetic Blessing is permanent, for God declared there will always be a Levite to serve Him (Jeremiah 33:21–22).

It is the grace of God that has transformed every person reading this book; we are a nation of kings and priests unto God. When I look across my congregation and see converted adulterers, drunkards, drug addicts, thieves, and self-righteous modern-day Pharisees, I see grace, mercy, and forgiveness in action.

There is a new beginning for everyone: "For all have sinned and fall short of the glory of God" (Romans 3:23). Is there secret sin in your past? Is there a dark page lurking in your history you don't like to think about and never talk about?

Confess it now! Let this day be the best day of the rest of your life! Become a new creature with an unlimited future. Don't allow Satan to hold you hostage to your sinful past any longer. Freedom is only a prayer away, but you must take the first step . . . I encourage you to do it now!

Judah

Leah's fourth son, Judah, slowly takes his place before his father as Simeon and Levi slip into a distant corner of the room to consider their future.

Judah's mind is warring within him. Which transgression would his father choose to display before his brothers? Would Jacob say anything about his pagan wife and the sons he had with her (Genesis 38:1–5)? Maybe it was the lie he told his daughter-in-law Tamar (Genesis 38:11, 14)? Or could it be that he made Tamar pregnant during one of his out-of-town trips? Judah was not the portrait of purity. Picture Tamar sitting by the roadside disguised as a prostitute. Judah stops and lusts after her; he goes into her tent and commits adultery with her, resulting in her conceiving a child (Genesis 38:18). Silent, as sweat beads on his brow, Judah waits.

Standing before the aged patriarch, Judah can almost hear the executioner's ax whirl past his ear as it approaches his neck. Judah remembers acknowledging his sin with Tamar (Genesis 38:26), but his thoughts are interrupted as Jacob begins to speak his Prophetic Blessing over him. Judah holds his breath as the Holy Spirit speaks through his father, who gives the first element of Judah's blessing:

Judah, you are he whom your brothers shall praise . . .
Your father's children shall bow down before you. (Genesis 49:8)

Judah is stunned! What did Jacob just say? Jacob makes absolutely no mention of Judah's decadent past. How can this be? Why no verbal parade of transgressions? What did Judah do to avoid judgment and merit this mind-boggling Prophetic Blessing?

Why would his father's children bow down before him? The Holy Spirit had revealed to Jacob the Divine lineage of Judah. The origin of Judah's name was his mother's expression of gratitude to God at his birth. However, Jacob saw the praise of a more noteworthy mother who would exalt the God of Abraham, Isaac, and Jacob for a greater Son that would come from the tribe of Judah.

And Mary said:
"My soul magnifies the Lord,
And my spirit has rejoiced in God my Savior
For He has regarded the lowly state of His maidservant;
For behold, henceforth all generations will call me blessed.

For He who is mighty has done great things for me
And holy is His name.
And His mercy is on those who fear Him
From generation to generation." (Luke 1:46–50)

God had elected that out of the loins of Judah would come the Lord Jesus Christ: "At the name of Jesus every knee should bow . . . and . . . every tongue should confess that Jesus Christ is Lord, to the glory of God the Father" (Philippians 2:10–11).

Second, Jacob says to Judah: "Your hand shall be on the neck of your enemies" (Genesis 49:8).

The Prophetic Blessing Fulfilled

The vast dominion of the tribe of Judah began in the days of King David, when he united a scattered kingdom and made Jerusalem the eternal capital of Israel. David's reign was the golden age of Israel.

Currently, Israel is surrounded by hostile nations who declare that the Israelites have no right to the land and, in the end, no right to exist.

As mentioned within Ezekiel's account of the future of Israel, Russia and Iran will lead Ethiopia, Libya, Germany, and Turkey in a land invasion of Israel (Ezekiel 38). This is known as the War of Gog and Magog. Russia will give military leadership to this anti-Israel axis of evil. God will allow this union to form an army and begin their trek toward

Israel—Israel, His beloved, His land of covenant given to Abraham, Isaac, and Jacob and their seed forever by blood covenant (Genesis 15).

But the moment the invading armies put their feet on Israel's soil, God will put His foot on the neck of Israel's enemies and crush them. Five out of six of Israel's enemies will be destroyed supernaturally (Ezekiel 39:2 KJV) in the most dramatic display of supernatural power against Israel's enemies since God turned Pharaoh and his army into fish food at the bottom of the Red Sea.

Next, Jacob identifies the symbol of the tribe of Judah as a lion: "Judah is a lion's whelp" (Genesis 49:9), fulfilled when Jesus Christ Himself announces that He is "the Lion of the tribe of Judah" (Revelation 5:5).

The fourth element of Jacob's prophetic proclamation concerning Judah is one of the most powerful utterances of Prophetic Blessing ever given in Scripture. The aged patriarch leans on his walking stick, his piercing eyes focused upon his son Judah, as the *Shekinah glory of God* gives him the revelation of events to take place centuries in the future:

> *The scepter shall not depart from Judah,*
> *Nor a lawgiver from between his feet,*
> *Until Shiloh comes;*
> *And to Him shall be the obedience of the people. (Genesis 49:10)*

The Hebrew term for *scepter* is translated "tribe" in verses 16 and 28 of this chapter and signifies the tribal rod or staff, which represents tribal authority. This fourth element in Jacob's Prophetic Blessing reveals that, at some point in the future, the authority of the tribe of Judah would cease to exist, but only after Shiloh (peace), the Prince of Peace—Messiah—has appeared.[4]

Dramatically, this Prophetic Blessing was fulfilled exactly, as evidenced in John 18:31: "Then Pilate said to them, 'You [the Jewish people, the tribe of Judah] take Him [Jesus] and judge Him according to your law.'" Now, listen closely to the response of the Jewish leaders: "Therefore the Jews said to him [Pilate], 'It is not lawful for us to put anyone to death.'" The Jewish leaders confessed they had no authority to put anyone to death. By their own confession, they were under Roman authority, and Genesis 49:10 was fulfilled.

No longer were they under their own authority; they were under Rome's authority. That could not happen until Shiloh, the Messiah, appeared. The Messiah was, in fact, standing before them, on trial for His life under Roman authority; it was Jesus of Nazareth, the root of the house of David and Shiloh Himself.

Jacob closes his prophetic utterance to Judah by saying:

Binding his donkey to the vine,
And his donkey's colt to the choice vine,
He washed his garments in wine,

And his clothes in the blood of grapes.
His eyes are darker than wine,
And his teeth whiter than milk. (Genesis 49:11–12)

Who is Jacob talking about? What is the Holy Spirit show-ing him that will happen centuries in the future?

Jacob is talking about Jesus Christ riding into Jerusalem on a donkey, offering Himself as the Lamb of God slain from the foundations of the earth.

Jacob reaches over, puts his hands on Judah's shoulder, and whispers, "He washed his garments in wine" (Genesis 49:11). What kind of wine? Blood—His own cleansing blood![5]

When Christ comes the second time, His garments will be red with blood, but this time the blood will be from the enemies of Israel. This is confirmed in Isaiah 63:1–2:

Who is this who comes from Edom,
With dyed garments from Bozrah,
This One who is glorious in His apparel,
Traveling in the greatness of His strength? . . .
Why is Your apparel red,
And Your garments like one who treads in the winepress?

When Jacob saw Judah, he did not see his transgressions; they were blotted out. When Jacob's feeble eyes looked upon his son, all his spirit could see was the coming King. When Jacob saw Judah, all his spirit could see was the Messiah who died as a Lamb for our sins and resurrected as a Lion conquering the enemies of Israel, conquering death, hell, and the grave. All Jacob's spirit could see was Jesus Christ, the Savior of Mankind.

Zebulun

Judah walks away from Jacob's bedside, his mind spinning with the cryptic yet powerful prophecies spoken over him by his father, Jacob. His mind asks the same question over and over: *How can this be?*

Zebulun, Leah's sixth son, approaches the judgment seat of Jacob. The youngest of Leah's sons stands quietly, not knowing what to expect. Jacob pronounces his blessings:

> *Zebulun shall dwell by the haven of the sea;*
> *He shall become a haven for ships,*
> *And his border shall adjoin Sidon. (Genesis 49:13)*

The Prophetic Blessing Fulfilled

The members of the tribe of Zebulun were a people "who jeopardized their lives to the point of death" (Judge 5:18) in Israel's victory over Jabin and Sisera. The people of Zebulun, "such as went forth to battle, expert in war, with all instruments of war, fifty thousand, which could keep rank: they were not of double heart" (1 Chronicles 12:33 KJV).

Zebulun was to be a commercial and seafaring tribe. When Jacob said, "His border shall adjoin Sidon," which was in Phoenicia, he implied that Zebulun would take part in Phoenician commerce.

The tribe of Zebulun was comprised of working people. When there was a job to be done, the descendants of Zebulun rolled up their sleeves and went to work. The Bible records that the tribe of Zebulun was "bringing food on donkeys and camels, on mules and oxen—provisions of flour and cakes of figs and cakes of raisins, wine and oil and oxen and sheep abundantly, for there was joy in Israel" (1 Chronicles 12:40).

The land in Israel that was given to the tribe of Zebulun, together with Naphtali, was known as the "Galilee of the Gentiles" (Matthew 4:15). It is to be noted that eleven out of the twelve disciples of Jesus were from Galilee. Jacob closes his Prophetic Blessing over Zebulun saying: "He shall become a haven for ships" (Genesis 49:13).

Galilee was to provide a refuge, a harbor, a place where storm-tossed ships could anchor at rest. It was here that Joseph and Mary, with the child Jesus, found a haven after their return from Egypt. Galilee was a refuge for Jesus after He began His ministry, as verified by John 7:1: "After these things Jesus walked in Galilee; for He did not want to walk in Judea, because the Jews sought to kill Him."

Galilee was a haven of rest for the Son of God as prophesied by Jacob thousands of years before Jesus walked on the shores of the Sea of Galilee with His message of hope and redemption.

Jacob's withered hand drops from Zebulun's head, and his future, as well as that of the thousands who would come from his loins, is etched in history foretold.[6]

Issachar

Issachar, Leah's fifth son, takes his turn to receive Jacob's Prophetic Blessing. Jacob, moving by the Shekinah of God, speaks the following words:

> *Issachar is a strong donkey,*
> *Lying down between two burdens;*
> *He saw that rest was good,*
> *And that the land was pleasant;*
> *He bowed his shoulder to bear a burden,*
> *And became a band of slaves. (Genesis 49:14–15)*

The Prophetic Blessing Fulfilled

The tribe of Issachar was located in the northern part of Israel. They were a working people who enjoyed their connection to the land.

When Jacob looked at his son, he spoke of his great strength, saying, "Issachar is a strong donkey" (Genesis 49:14). Being compared to a donkey may not sound too flattering today, but in ancient Israel, an ass or donkey was looked upon as an honorable and loyal animal ready to do its master's bidding.

It must be remembered that Israel had no horses until

the reign of King Solomon. God prohibited the Israelites from raising horses to prevent Israel from returning quickly to Egypt (Deuteronomy 17:16).

The donkey was a reminder to Israel that they were a separated people whose trust was in the Lord, not in horses and chariots.[7] The tribe of Issachar was numbered at eighty-seven thousand "mighty men of valor" (1 Chronicles 7:5) who were ready and willing to do God's bidding.

Life is for one generation. A good name is forever! The tribe of Issachar has forever been remembered as "mighty men of valor"!

Dan, Gad, Asher, and Naphtali

Jacob motions with his trembling hand for Dan, Naphtali, Gad, and Asher to come forward. These are the sons born of the servants Bilah and Zilpah. In ancient Israel, it was permitted for the wife to give her husband a servant as a concubine in order to have children. This is what Sarah did in presenting Hagar to Abraham. To be born of a concubine was not in the same social standing as being born of a wife.

There are people reading this book who feel insignificant for a variety of reasons. Some, like these brothers, may grieve over the circumstances of their birth. Some come from broken homes and were raised by aunts, uncles, grandparents, or by state agencies.

Some come from homes wrecked by spousal abuse, divorce, drugs, or alcoholism. They lived from day-to-day not knowing what tomorrow would bring. Some presently live under the cloud of not knowing their roots, with a longing to know their birth parents.

But the Great I AM, the Creator of heaven and earth, the Father of Abraham, Isaac, and Jacob, loves us all no matter how severely scarred our lives may be.

Dan, Gad, Asher, and Naphtali stand before Jacob wondering if they will even be included in the Prophetic Blessings—and they are! "In truth I perceive that God shows no partiality" (Acts 10:34). We are all one in Christ. There should never be any feeling of inferiority or superiority among the body of Christ; we are one family with one Lord, one faith, and one baptism.

Dan

> *Dan shall judge his people*
> *As one of the tribes of Israel.*
> *Dan shall be a serpent by the way,*
> *A viper by the path,*
> *That bites the horse's heels*
> *So that its rider shall fall backward.*
> *I have waited for your salvation, O LORD! (Genesis 49:16–18)*

The Prophetic Blessing Fulfilled
Jacob's prophetic vision that "Dan shall judge his people as one of the tribes of Israel" was accurate, for out of Dan came

the mightiest judge in all of Israel—Samson—whose exploits became a legend in Israel.[8]

But before Dan can wipe the relieved smile from his face, the aged voice of Jacob cuts like a saber: "Dan shall be a serpent by the way, a viper by the path, that bites the horse's heels so that its rider shall fall backward."

It was the tribe of Dan that first introduced idolatry into Israel (Judges 18:30–31), and it was within Dan that Jeroboam set up one of his golden calves (1 Kings 12:2–30). But the Holy Spirit revealed one last element for Dan—pardon! "I have waited for your salvation, O LORD!" (Genesis 49:18).

It should be noted that the words "I have waited for your salvation, O LORD" are the first reference to salvation in the Bible. And it occurs in connection to Dan.[9] Jacob, peering through the telescope of time, declares that the Lord, the God who keeps covenant for a thousand generations, will bring salvation even to Dan with his serpent-like ways. Jacob spoke of grace in the midst of judgment, forgiveness in the midst of transgression, and redemption in the midst of death. Salvation, grace, forgiveness, and redemption are available to all of us for the asking. "Ask, and it will be given to you" (Luke 11:9).

Gad

The room is silent as Gad steps forward. Jacob's voice, though weak, is filled with God's anointing. All of Gad's brothers listen intently to hear their father's proclamation over Gad:

Gad, a troop shall tramp upon him,
But he shall triumph at last. (Genesis 49:19)

The Prophetic Blessing Fulfilled

Jacob saw Gad both conquered and triumphant. The tribe of Gad would be in a constant state of warfare. However, Gad had its superstars, including Elijah, the prince of the prophets, who challenged Ahab and Jezebel and their cadre of false prophets, calling down a drought for three and a half years that ended in a theological shoot-out at the Old Testament *OK Corral* called Mount Carmel.

Gad was both a warrior and an overcomer, a man who took action in a day when actions determined the destiny of men and nations. Your actions will determine your destiny! The world is full of doers and dreamers; those who choose to take action, seize the moment, and control their lives. Take charge of your life or someone else will!

Asher

It is now Asher's turn to stand before the judgment seat of Jacob; all are still present in the room awaiting the final utterance of the patriarch. So shall it be, according to St. Paul: "We must all appear before the judgment seat of Christ, that each one may receive the things done in the body, according to what he has done, whether good or bad" (2 Corinthians 5:10).

Jacob's piercing glare focuses like a laser beam on Asher

as the Holy Spirit begins to reveal his future. Jacob sees life's rewards and royal riches for his son Asher.

Bread from Asher shall be rich,
And he shall yield royal dainties. (Genesis 49:20)

The Prophetic Blessing Fulfilled

How Asher must have smiled with joy and relief over his Prophetic Blessing. The proclamation "bread from Asher shall be rich" was fulfilled in the days of famine when God sent Elijah to the house of the widow in Zarepath, saying, "See, I have commanded a widow there to provide for you" (1 Kings 17:9). Zarepath was in Sidon, and Sidon was in Asher's territory (Joshua 19:28).

The Prophetic Blessing "he shall yield royal dainties" was fulfilled when Anna—age eighty-four, a prophetess, the daughter of Phanuel, of the tribe of Asher, who served the Lord in the temple day and night—offered a blessed *dainty* to Israel's newborn King, Jesus Christ, when He was brought to the temple.[10]

Luke records that when Anna saw Jesus being brought into the temple, "*She gave thanks to the Lord, and spoke of Him to all* those who looked for redemption in Jerusalem" (Luke 2:36–38).

In Acts 27, the apostle Paul was being carried as a prisoner to Rome, and when the ship reached Sidon (the border of Asher), "Julius treated Paul kindly and gave him liberty to go to his friends and receive care" (v. 3). This, again, is an example of bread out of Asher.

It was prophesied that Asher was to "dip his foot in oil" (Deuteronomy 33:24). Bible scholars are focused on the rich oil-producing olive groves that flourish so abundantly in Asher's territory. But there's more, much more!

The modern port of Haifa is situated in Asher's territory, and the giant pipelines from Middle Eastern oil fields terminate in Asher's territory.

Also, the *New York Times* reported that one of the world's largest gas fields was recently discovered off the coast of Haifa (Asher's territory).

> Houston-based Noble Energy, which is working with several Israeli partner companies, said that the field, named Leviathan, whose existence was suspected months ago, has at least 16 trillion cubic feet of gas at a likely market value of tens of billions of dollars and should turn Israel into an energy exporter.[11]

Asher is indeed "dipping his foot in oil."

Naphtali

Jacob now receives Naphtali, the last son of his maidservants. Jacob brings attention first to Naphtali's natural wildness, saying:

Naphtali is a deer let loose;
He uses beautiful words. (Genesis 49:21)

The Prophetic Blessing Fulfilled

The King James Version says, "Naphtali is a hind let loose: he giveth goodly words." The word *hind* describes a female deer, a timid, swift, and graceful creature of the woods. In Naphtali's early years, he had apparently been a wild, graceful, and uncontrolled young man.

Some scholars suggest that when the brothers returned from Egypt with the news that Joseph was alive, Naphtali ran ahead to tell his father (Jacob) not only that all was well with Benjamin but also that Joseph lived.[12]

Later, in the war against Sisera during the time of Deborah, the courageous warriors of Naphtali, including Barak, were aggressive and as swift as lightning, playing an integral part in this victory (Judges 4).

The second element of Naphtali's Prophetic Blessing was "he uses beautiful words." He was a man of excellent speech—an orator.

As Naphtali stood before the dying Jacob, I'm sure Jacob recalled the scene of graceful, swift Naphtali running toward him across the green pasture, bringing beautiful words: "All is well and Joseph lives!"

At Jacob's judgment seat, Naphtali's swiftness of foot and beautiful words brought forth Jacob's expression of love and praise. At the judgment seat of Christ, may our *walk* and our *talk* bring an expression of approval from Jehovah God: "Well done, good and faithful servant" (Matthew 25:21).

Joseph

Jacob's blessing of Joseph is saturated with blessings both natural and supernatural. Listen as the patriarch speaks; his words ring true over the centuries:

> *Joseph is a fruitful bough,*
> *A fruitful bough by a well;*
> *His branches run over the wall.*
> *The archers have bitterly grieved him,*
> *Shot at him and hated him.*
> *But his bow remained in strength,*
> *And the arms of his hands were made strong*
> *By the hands of the Mighty God of Jacob*
> *(From there is the Shepherd, the Stone of Israel),*
> *By the God of your father who will help you,*
> *And by the Almighty who will bless you*
> *With blessings of heaven above,*
> *Blessings of the deep that lies beneath,*
> *Blessings of the breasts and of the womb.*
> *The blessings of your father*
> *Have excelled the blessings of my ancestors,*
> *Up to the utmost bound of the everlasting hills.*
> *They shall be on the head of Joseph,*
> *And on the crown of the head of him who was separate*
> *from his brothers. (Genesis 49:22–26)*

The Prophetic Blessing Fulfilled

One of the most magnificent prophetic overlays in Scripture involves the similarities between the life of Joseph and the life of Jesus. Only a book of supernatural origins could foreshadow such a revelation.

⅋ THINK ᴏɴ THIS ⅋

The Old Testament is God's will *concealed*;
the New Testament is God's will *revealed*.

1. Both Joseph and Jesus were the favorite sons of their fathers.

Now Israel loved Joseph more than all his children, because he was the son of his old age. (Genesis 37:3)

The Word became flesh and made his dwelling among us. We have seen his glory, the glory of the One and Only, who came from the Father, full of grace and truth. (John 1:14 NIV1984)

2. Joseph was given a robe of many colors, which the Old Testament says was fitting for royalty.

Also [Israel] made [Joseph] a tunic of many colors. (Genesis 37:3)

Jesus was given a seamless robe because He w̶.̶ ̶.̶o̶y̶alty

—*the King of kings, and the Lord of lords, and the Prince of Peace.*

Now the tunic was without seam, woven from the top in one piece. (John 19:23)

Pilate had a notice prepared and fastened to the cross. It read: JESUS OF NAZARETH, THE KING OF THE JEWS. (John 19:19 NIV1984)

3. Joseph was sent by his father with food for his brothers in the field.

Please go and see if it is well with your brothers and well with the flocks, and bring back word to me. (Genesis 37:14)

Jesus was sent by God the Father to the earth as the Bread of Life and Living Water.

For the bread of God is He who comes down from heaven and gives life to the world. (John 6:33)

4. Joseph was rejected by his brothers.

Now when they saw him afar off, even before he came near them, they conspired against him to kill him. (Genesis 37:18)

Jesus was rejected by His brothers.

He came unto his own, and his own received him not. (John 1:11 KJV)

5. *Joseph was sold by his brothers for the price of a slave.*

. . . [The brothers] sold him to the Ishmaelites for twenty shekels of silver. And they took Joseph to Egypt. (Genesis 37:28)

Jesus was sold by a disciple for thirty pieces of silver, the price of a slave.

"What are you willing to give me if I deliver Him to you?" And they counted out to him thirty pieces of silver. (Matthew 26:15)

6. *Joseph was falsely accused of rape by Potiphar's desperate housewife and sent to prison.*

So it happened, as I lifted my voice and cried out, that he left his garment with me and fled outside. (Genesis 39:18)

Jesus was falsely accused by the Pharisees of being a demonized heretic, a drunkard, and a madman.

The Jews answered Him, saying, "For a good work we do not stone You, but for blasphemy, and because You, being a Man, make Yourself God." (John 10:33)

7. *Joseph was sent to prison, where he came out on a day certain to stand at the right hand of the most powerful man on earth, Pharaoh, as prime minister of Egypt.*

Then Pharaoh sent and called Joseph, and they brought him quickly out of the dungeon; and he shaved, changed his clothing, and came to Pharaoh. . . . "You shall be over my house, and all my people shall be ruled according to your word; only in regard to the throne will I be greater than you." (Genesis 41:14, 40)

Jesus was sent into the prison of the grave where He came out on a day certain, the third day, to stand at the right hand of the most powerful force in the universe, God Almighty, as the Prince of Glory.

Then, as they were afraid and bowed their faces to the earth, they said to them, "Why do you seek the living among the dead? He is not here, but is risen! Remember how He spoke to you when He was still in Galilee, saying, 'The Son of Man must be delivered into the hands of sinful men, and be crucified, and the third day rise again.'" (Luke 24:5–7)

8. Joseph, who was Jewish, was given an Egyptian wife who was a Gentile. They had two sons, Manasseh and Ephraim, who shared equally in the inheritance of the land of Israel.

And Pharaoh called Joseph's name . . . and he gave him as a wife Asenath, the daughter of Poti-Pherah priest of On. (Genesis 41:45)

Jesus, a Jewish rabbi, was given a Gentile bride at the cross. At the cross, the Gentiles were made to be heirs and joint heirs with Jesus Christ.

And if some of the branches were broken off, and you, being a wild olive tree, were grafted in among them, and with them became a partaker of the root and fatness of the olive tree. (Romans 11:17)

9. Joseph, through revelation knowledge, told his generation the future of the world, which saved Egypt and the Jewish people from starvation.

So all countries came to Joseph in Egypt to buy grain, because the famine was severe in all lands. (Genesis 41:57)

Jesus told His followers the future of Israel, which is the backbone of prophecy. Then He told the church the future of the world in the book of Revelation through the pen of the apostle John.

Tell us, when will these things be? And what will be the sign of Your coming, and of the end of the age? (Matthew 24:3)

The Revelation of Jesus Christ, which God gave Him to show His servants—things which must shortly take place. (Revelation 1:1)

10. Joseph's brothers went to Egypt three times searching for food. It was on the third visit that Joseph revealed himself as their brother, saying, "I am Joseph."

First time: So Joseph's ten brothers went down to buy grain in Egypt. (Genesis 42:3)

Second time: Go back, buy us a little food. (Genesis 43:2)

Third time: So Judah and his brothers came to Joseph's house, and he was still there; and they fell before him on the ground. (Genesis 44:14)

Then Joseph said to his brothers, "I am Joseph; does my father still live?" (Genesis 45:3)

In the history of Israel, the Jewish people have now entered the land of Israel for the third time in their history.
The first time was with Joshua just after the death of Moses.
Moses My servant is dead. Now therefore, arise, go over this Jordan, you and all this people, to the land which I am giving to them—the children of Israel. (Joshua 1:2)

The second time was their return from Babylon.
Now these are the people of the province who came back from the captivity, of those who had been carried away, whom Nebuchadnezzar the king of Babylon had

carried away to Babylon, and who returned to Jerusalem and Judah, everyone to his own city. (Ezra 2:1)

The third time was May 15, 1948, when Israel was reborn in a day.

Who has heard such a thing?
Who has seen such things?
Shall the earth be made to give birth in one day?
Or shall a nation be born at once?
For as soon as Zion was in labor,
She gave birth to her children. (Isaiah 66:8)

The important fact to remember is that on the third time into the land, Messiah will reveal Himself to the Jewish people, saying, "I am Jesus!"
And I will pour on the house of David and on the inhabitants of Jerusalem the Spirit of grace and supplication; then they will look on Me whom they pierced. Yes, they will mourn for Him as one mourns for his only son, and grieve for Him as one grieves for a firstborn. (Zechariah 12:10)

11. Before Joseph revealed himself to his brothers, he asked the Egyptians to leave the room.
Then Joseph could not restrain himself before all those who stood by him, and he cried out, "Make everyone go out from me!" (Genesis 45:1)

Before Jesus Christ reveals Himself to His own, the church will be raptured.

Then we who are alive and remain shall be caught up together with them in the clouds to meet the Lord in the air. And thus we shall always be with the Lord. (1 Thessalonians 4:17)

12. How did Joseph prove he was their brother? How could they be certain he was related to them? Egyptians did not circumcise their sons. Joseph showed his brothers his circumcision.

So no one stood with him while Joseph made himself known to his brothers. (Genesis 45:1)

How will Jesus prove He is the Messiah? He will show them His pierced side.

Then they will look on Me whom they pierced. Yes, they will mourn for Him as one mourns for his only son, and grieve for Him as one grieves for a firstborn. (Zechariah 12:10)

The Hebrew word for "pierced" means "riven side."

13. What was the emotional reaction of Joseph's brothers when the scales fell from their eyes and they recognized Joseph?

But his brothers could not answer him, for they were dismayed in his presence. (Genesis 45:3)

What will be the reaction of the Jewish people when they see and fully recognize Jesus as the Messiah at His second coming? The prophet Zechariah described a week of national mourning in Israel expressing the deepest of sorrow.

Yes, they will mourn for Him as one mourns for his only son, and grieve for Him as one grieves for a first-born. In that day there shall be a great mourning in Jerusalem, like the mourning at Hadad Rimmon in the plain of Megiddo. And the land shall mourn, every family by itself: the family of the house of David by itself, and their wives by themselves; the family of the house of Nathan by itself, and their wives by them-selves . . . all the families that remain, every family by itself, and their wives by themselves. (Zechariah 12:10–14)

14. What was Joseph's reaction when his brothers started weeping?

But now, do not therefore be grieved or angry with yourselves because you sold me here; for God sent me before you to preserve life. (Genesis 45:5)

But as for you, you meant evil against me; but God

meant it for good, in order to bring it about as it is this day, to save many people alive. (Genesis 50:20)

15. What will God Almighty do when the Jewish people recognize Jesus for who He really is?
And I will pour on the house of David and on the inhabitants of Jerusalem the Spirit of grace and supplication. (Zechariah 12:10)

⍟ THINK ON THIS ⍟

Think on this: Both Joseph and Jesus were sent to their brothers to provide for their salvation. God's future plan for Israel is grace and mercy.[13]

Benjamin

Benjamin is the son of Jacob's old age, born in the same hour that Rachel, the love of his life, died. Jacob lovingly extends his trembling hand toward his beloved son. When his hand is on his head, he says:

Benjamin is a ravenous wolf;
In the morning he shall devour the prey,
And at night he shall divide the spoil. (Genesis 49:27)

When I participated in sports at George Washington Middle School in Houston, Texas, our mascot was a ravenous wolf. The wolf is the largest and fiercest of the canine family, weighing as much as one hundred pounds. It is a relentless predator.

It is the relentless and ravenous wolf that Jacob sees in the future for his youngest son. Benjamin would become a warrior tribe in Israel.

The Prophetic Blessing Fulfilled

So they arose and went over by number, twelve from Benjamin, followers of Ishbosheth the son of Saul, and twelve from the servants of David. And each one grasped his opponent by the head and thrust his sword in his opponent's side; so they fell down [dead] together. (2 Samuel 2:15–16)

Benjamin's descendants were fierce warriors as depicted in the story of the concubine at Gibeah (Judges 19–20). Other distinguished warriors were King Saul, who rose as Israel's champion during the early years of Israel's history by defeating Moab, Edom, and Philistia (1 Samuel 14:47); Queen Esther and Mordecai, who defeated Haman (Esther 8:7)[14]; and Saul of Tarsus, who became the apostle Paul, whose fierce and relentless warrior instincts established the New Testament church and eventually the fall of the Roman Empire. All were descendants of Benjamin.

St. Paul's final farewell to the church offers a true portrait of a Benjamite:

I have fought the good fight, I have finished the race. (2 Timothy 4:7)

You therefore must endure hardship as a good soldier of Jesus Christ. (2 Timothy 2:3)

The relentless dispositions of the descendants of the tribe of Benjamin were set in motion by the power of Jacob's prophetic proclamation.

THE GREAT EXCHANGE AT THE CROSS

The Roman government considered Jesus Christ an enemy of the state and sentenced Him to be crucified as an insurrectionist too dangerous to live. The Romans were masters of brutality; they had perfected crucifixion. At one time in their history, they crucified two thousand Jews at once to demonstrate their cruel malice.

I want you to imagine yourself sitting at the base of the cross at Calvary. Jesus Christ is hanging on the blood-soaked cross; above His head is a crude sign reading "King of the Jews." Envision His brutally beaten body, ripped apart by thirty-nine stripes—leaving His back a bloody mass of twisted flesh and exposed bone. Can you see the Roman spittle dripping from His beard, put there by the soldiers who taunted the King of kings as He stood silent before them?

Watch as He hangs completely naked between two thieves. Who would be foolish enough to follow this humiliated rebel from Galilee? Can you hear His moaning as He writhes in pain? Picture His body heaving up and down as He struggles for breath. Christ could kill every Roman soldier with one spoken word. Instead He cries out to His Father, "My God, My God, why have You forsaken Me?" (Mark 15:34).

In response to His Son's desperate cry, God remains silent. Instead God the Father extends His right hand of blessing to the Gentiles, "who were without Christ, being aliens from the commonwealth of Israel and strangers from the covenants of promise, having no hope and without God in the world" (Ephesians 2:12).

Jesus Christ of Nazareth was the Firstborn of God the Father. He deserved the right hand of blessing. But on this day—a day when the sun refuses to shine at high noon—God places His right hand on the Gentiles, giving us the greater blessing.

The most accurate description of what was accomplished at the cross that day was given by the prophet Isaiah seven hundred years before it took place: "All we like sheep have gone astray; we have turned, every one, to his own way; and the LORD has laid on Him the iniquity of us all" (Isaiah 53:6).

God the Father initiated the Great Exchange when He placed His right hand of greater blessing on the Gentiles and then placed His left hand on the brow of His suffering Son.

- Jesus was punished that we, as Gentiles, might be forgiven (Isaiah 53:4–5).

- Jesus was wounded that we might be healed—He took upon Himself our sicknesses and diseases as we received divine health (Isaiah 53:4–5; Psalm 103:3).
- Jesus took our sin, and we received God's total and immediate forgiveness (2 Corinthians 5:21).
- Jesus took our poverty at the cross so that we may receive the riches of Abraham (2 Corinthians 8:9).
- Jesus endured our rejection that we might be accepted by the Father: "And about the ninth hour Jesus cried out with a loud voice, saying . . . 'My God, My God, why have You forsaken Me?'" (Matthew 27:46, 50). For the first time, the Son of God called out to His Father and received no response. He was rejected because our sin was upon Him.
- Jesus died that we might have everlasting life (Romans 6:23).

Many reading this book are suffering from some form of rejection. You were rejected by one or both of your parents. You were rejected by your spouse who left you for someone else. You were rejected by your dearest friend, and the wounds are too deep to heal. I have good news! Jesus has borne your rejection. He took it from you at the cross and has given you the joy and blessing of the Lord, which "makes one rich, and He adds no sorrow with it" (Proverbs 10:22).[15]

The crossed hands of Jacob were a type and foreshadowing of the day at the cross when God the Father gave to us, as Gentiles, the best blessing and gave to His Son our sin, our sickness, our poverty, our rejection, our shame. God adopted us as sons and daughters in His kingdom, which shall never end.

⚜ THINK ON THIS ⚜

The message of the cross is the central theme of the Word of God. The day of the cross was the day of shame for Jesus Christ; it was the day of redemption for every believer. It was the Great Exchange.

CHAPTER SEVEN

THE EIGHT PROPHETIC BLESSINGS OF JESUS

Blessed are . . .

—MATTHEW 5:3–12

It is God's passionate desire to bless you. It was in the genesis of time that a loving and gracious God created a garden of such splendor that the mind of man cannot begin to imagine the half of its grandeur. He created Adam and Eve, and immediately gave to them the blessing of His unmerited favor.

He later called Abram out of the land of Ur and bestowed upon him the Prophetic Blessings remaining with his descendants now and forever:

Now the LORD had said to Abram . . .
"I will bless those who bless you,

And I will curse him who curses you;
And in you all the families of the earth shall be blessed."
(Genesis 12:1, 3)

Then Jacob, the patriarch, called his twelve sons on the day of his death and blessed them as he sat on his bed and leaned on his walking stick. The power of the Prophetic Blessing was passed to those twelve sons, as history was foretold in the mouth of this beloved patriarch.

Generations later came a rabbi by the name of Jesus of Nazareth, born in a Bethlehem manger on a holy night while angels sang and shepherds came to pay homage to the King of the Jews. At the beginning of His ministry, Jesus pronounced eight Prophetic Blessings upon which the kingdom of God would be forever established.

"JESUS IS COMING!"

Join me on the grassy slopes of the mountain that forms the banks of the Sea of Galilee. Let's step back in time more than two thousand years and stand with the multitudes that await the arrival of this newly celebrated rabbi and His twelve disciples.

It's a hot, sultry day as the sweltering wind spins dust clouds and carries them swiftly down the winding road to the Sea of Galilee. Yet there's an air of expectancy in the atmosphere. Listen as voices rise to an excited, feverish pitch as friend calls a greeting to friend. Along every trail leading from Galilee, small groups of people begin to gather. The word has spread that Jesus is coming.

Suddenly He and His small band of followers emerge over the brow of a slight hill on the Capernaum road, and immediately in their wake is a vast multitude of people from Decapolis, Jerusalem, Judea, and beyond Jordan.

The word continues to spread from person to person. "Jesus is coming!" Crowds from Tiberius, Bethsaida, and Capernaum soon join the others. Together they follow Jesus and the twelve simple men who would, in time, turn the world upside down. As they reach the summit of the hill, the gentle winds from the plains sweep over them, affording relief from the sun's scorching heat. Jesus stops and motions for them to sit down and rest.

The air is electric. It is a moment to be captured and held for eternity. The masses begin to quiet as Jesus gets ready to speak. Silence falls upon the gathering as people gaze expectantly at this rabbi from Nazareth.

What He says on this day in ancient Israel will go down in history as the most inspirational and profound truths ever spoken. In reverent, measured, modest words, He reveals the secret of joy, the secret of victory over worry-free living, ultimately the secrets of the good life—they are the eight Prophetic Blessings that are the constitution of the kingdom of God.

The first word Jesus used in His address is reported by Matthew this way: "Then He opened his mouth and taught them, saying, '*Blessed . . !*'" (Matthew 5:2–3). As Jesus opened His mouth, the *ruach* (supernatural breath) came forth just as it did in the Garden of Eden when God the Father breathed life into Adam. Now the *ruach* of His Son would bless the people with eight life-changing Prophetic Blessings.

God wants to bless all men. His greatest glory is to bring joy unspeakable, love, and peace to all who will become a part of the kingdom of God.

To be blessed of God is the central theme of Christianity. This is the theme Jesus declared as He began His historic Sermon on the Mount. He mapped out the royal road for all men to be supremely blessed. He did not come to take away the joy of life with religious rules; He came to fill the cup of joy to overflowing and to hand it to all who are willing to be blessed.

The word *blessed* has become religious, musty, and remote. Many translate this word as *happy*, which is superficial in concept. *Happiness* comes from the Scandinavian word *hap*, from which we get the word *happenstance*.

That would imply that men can only be happy when the circumstances of life are happy. Briefly stated, you can only be happy as a result of happenstance. Happiness, therefore, depends on the things that happen to you by chance.

The Greek word *blessed* that Jesus used in the Beatitudes is *makarios*. It is not the word meaning happiness; it is the word used in classical Greek for the attainment of *summum bonum*—life's highest ideal.

Jesus, the Son of God who had all knowledge and wisdom, was offering His congratulations to the person who lives in the anointing of these eight Prophetic Blessings of the Sermon on the Mount. Jesus was actually saying to mortal flesh that if you are getting the best out of life, you are living the kind of life that's really worth living—you are living the good life!

Who is living the good life? Who is the man or the woman who lives with unspeakable joy and a deep peace unknown to other people? Who fully understands the secret of living life with unlimited favor? What kind of life releases the fountains of love that renew and refresh themselves every day?

THE SECRETS OF THE GOOD LIFE

The First Prophetic Blessing

> *Blessed are the poor in spirit,*
> *For theirs is the kingdom of heaven. (Matthew 5:3)*

Many reading this book know a distinct kind of poverty—the poverty of poor self-image. The Bible commands, "Love your neighbor as yourself" (Matthew 22:39). It's a fact: if you don't like yourself, you won't like your neighbor, your wife, or your children.

The ten spies who went into the Promised Land returned with a poor self-image. They spied out the Promised Land

and whimpered to Moses, "There we saw the giants . . . and we were like grasshoppers in our own sight" (Numbers 13:33).

The opposite of having poor self-image is being steeped in pride. You may not believe that happiness comes to the humble, but you can be certain it does not come to the proud.

In Luke 18, two men went up to the Temple to pray. One said, "God, I thank You that I am not like other men" (v. 11). He arrogantly announced his perceived good qualities and prayerfully proclaimed them to every person in the temple.

The other man prayed, "God, be merciful to me a sinner" (v. 13). The poverty that is key to God's kingdom is the realization that although we might possess all things, without God, all our things amount to nothing.

The prodigal son demanded that his father immediately give him his inheritance. This arrogant son was tired of keeping his father's stuffy rules. He knew how to live the good life; all he needed was the opportunity.

With his inheritance in his pocket, he leaped on his Harley-Davidson and headed for the big city. There, in a very short period of time, he lost all his wealth, his honor, and his good name.

He was hired to care for pigs, which for the Jewish people was the ultimate humiliation. As he fought the swine for food to eat, he came to himself and realized his true poverty. He stood up, scraped the mud off his clothes, and made a life-changing decision: "I will arise and go to my father" (Luke 15:18).

The prodigal son grasped that he needed his father. The type of humbleness that makes us prosperous *within* is the realization that we need God. This revelation knowledge leads us down the path of righteousness and true riches. The Bible says, "The blessing of the LORD makes one rich, and He adds no sorrow with it" (Proverbs 10:22).

Donald Trump and Warren Buffet are billionaires, but they cannot create the seed that makes a loaf of bread; they cannot produce lasting peace or purchase one more second when their time on this earth comes to an end. The richest families in the world were on the *Titanic* and could not control the crisis that took their lives. Riches cannot buy the good life!

Many believe that faith in God only offers self-denial in this life, with a "pie in the sky" promise for the future. Not so! Notice that Jesus used the verb *is*—"For theirs *is* the kingdom of heaven." His kingdom becomes the believer's *immediate* possession. And by possessing the kingdom, you possess all things. Possessing God's power enables us to face life with enthusiasm; it gives us a deep, inward peace because we are not afraid of tomorrow. We experience an inner joy that outward circumstances cannot provide us. Because God is within us, and because God is love, there flows out of us a love for others that sweeps away all prejudice, jealousy, and hate.

Blessed Are the Cracked Pots

My wife, Diana, illustrates a beautiful story told by Patsy Clairmont in her book *God Uses Cracked Pots.*[1] When she hosts her Women of God seminars, Diana displays two urn-shaped vases on a table. She takes a candle and places it in the first vase, which is beautiful and flawless in every way. Diana lights the candle, covers the opening of the vase, and holds it up for the audience to see. The vessel, though perfect, does not allow the light within it to shine through its unblemished exterior. It is useless to light a path for those needing to find their way.

Diana then places a candle in the second vase, which is cracked and scarred. She lights the candle, covers the opening, and holds up the ugly vessel. The radiant light from within the vessel floods through the broken places, providing a beautiful glow that guides those who have lost their way.

And so it is with our lives! We all have ugly cracks and scars caused from the heartbreaks of our past. Maybe those cracks and scars were caused by sexual abuse; perhaps they were caused by the rejection of your mother, your father, or even both your parents. Maybe those cracks were caused by a bitter divorce, or a secret abortion, or the time you spent in the penitentiary in the dark past no one knows about.

God, the Master Potter, could have allowed your life to be flawless—but those ugly cracks caused by the setbacks of life allow the light of God's love to shine through you to give guidance to those searching for truth in life's journey. Blessed are those who are *cracked pots,* whose imperfections of the past are the source of courage, strength, and inspiration for those searching for the Light of the world.

"I, Jesus, have sent My angel to testify to you these things in the churches. I am the Root and the Offspring of David, the Bright and Morning Star" (Revelation 22:16).

The Second Prophetic Blessing

Blessed are those who mourn,
For they shall be comforted. (Matthew 5:4)

The second Prophetic Blessing in the kingdom of God is mourning, which is even less attractive to us than poverty, yet only those who *feel* can mourn.

The apostle Paul wrote of people who are "past feeling" (Ephesians 4:19). He spoke of people "having their own conscience seared with a hot iron" (1 Timothy 4:2). They live in hypocrisy, and their conscience no longer pains their hearts.

Do you remember the story of Father Damien? He became a missionary to the lepers of the island of Molokai, Hawaii. For thirteen years, he shared their personal Gethsemane. For thirteen years, he was their teacher, companion, and true friend.

Eventually, the dreaded disease of leprosy laid hold of him. At first, he was not aware of it, but one morning he happened to spill boiling water on his foot.

"How painful," you say. No, there was not the slightest pain. The loss of feeling informed Father Damien that leprosy had entered his body—he was slowly dying.

There is a far greater loss than that of physical sensitivity; it is the loss of your spiritual sensitivity toward God. When you get to the place where you can sin and your conscience no longer hurts you, you are dying spiritually. You have seared your conscience with sin's hot iron.

You lie, and there is no pain. You commit adultery, and there is no sorrow over the broken covenant with your spouse. You steal from your employer; at first, your conscience pains you, but no more. God's voice has become silent. You have become addicted to pornography; at first, you felt guilt, but no more. The voice of God has been smothered by your consistent carnal choices. Your conscience is dead. Your heart has become stone. You think you're sophisticated, but the truth is, you are numbered among the walking dead.

Your hand passes over your Bible that is collecting dust on your coffee table and picks up the remote so you can watch the filth on television. You pray only in a time of crisis; you have no fellowship with God. You enter His house on Easter and Christmas; otherwise, you have no use for the Creator.

Your conscience is screaming, *I want to live and be in the presence of God!* Yet you are slowly assassinating your sense of right and wrong with every disobedient act. The Holy Spirit has pricked your conscience again and again, but now that inner voice has grown silent and God is far from you. You have suffocated the Spirit of God that once lived within you, and as a result your happiness is lost—living the good life becomes an impossibility.

In the courtyard of Pilate's judgment hall, Peter denied Christ. Think of it! Was his soul forever damned? No, for Scripture states, "So Peter went out and wept bitterly" (Luke 22:62). He mourned his sinful conduct before the Judge of all judges. On Resurrection morning, the angel at the empty tomb told Mary Magdalene, "Go, tell His disciples—and Peter" (Mark 16:7). God restored Peter.

Compare that scene to that of Judas, who sold out the Lord for thirty pieces of silver. See him as, by the light of the Roman soldier's torches, he approaches the Master in the garden. Look at the smirk on his face as he says, "Hail, master" (Matthew 26:49 KJV). His was a hard, cold, calloused, and premeditated sin. There was no mourning or remorse as he betrayed the Son of God.

Most reading this book would say, "I would never do that!" But the Bible says that whenever you willfully sin and refuse to mourn your sin, "[You] crucify . . . the Son of God afresh" (Hebrews 6:6 KJV).

The Bible speaks of different kinds of mourning. There are nine Greek verbs in the biblical text used to express degrees of grief. The word for *mourning* used in the Beatitudes is the most severe of the nine.

You may not have denied Christ, you may not have committed unconfessed sin, but you are still suffering. In the real world you will come face-to-face with sorrow and heartbreaking grief.

But for the believer . . . mourning is limited! The Bible

says, "Weeping may endure for a night, but joy comes in the morning" (Psalm 30:5). Are you mourning? Is your heart broken? Do tears flow endlessly from your eyes over some great sorrow? The mourning you are experiencing is limited; it *will* end because God's joy *will* come in the morning. The pain of your loved one's death *will* end.

There *will* be a resurrection morning when the dead in Christ shall rise. The pain of divorce *will* end; joy *will* come in the morning. The pain of financial reversal *will* end; God *will* provide and joy *will* come in the morning. The pain inflicted by your enemies *will* end, and joy *will* come in the morning.

A Soldier's Story

As a young evangelist in the early 1960s, I walked out on the platform of a small church in central Texas where I was a guest minister and looked out across a congregation of about two hundred people.

My eyes focused on a young soldier sitting in the back pew, just as close to the door as you could get and still be in the church. He sat ramrod straight, his hands folded in front of him as if he were standing at a military inspection. Even though he was young, his hair was white as snow and his youthful face was the portrait of pain and suffering. He looked as though he were being boiled in oil. Occasionally he would glance at the back door as if he were about to bolt through it to freedom and relief.

I preached that Sunday morning on the topic of shattered dreams. It was as if I had an audience of one—the other one hundred and ninety-nine were an audience of happenstance. I knew the message touched the soldier, but it did not move him enough to respond to the altar call.

As I stood on the front porch of the church with the host pastor, the sergeant's wife came through the doors first, dragging her husband behind her. He was obviously reluctant to meet the visiting preacher. You can tell a lot about a person by looking directly into their eyes. He had a story to tell, and I wanted to hear it. Why would someone so young have hair so white and eyes so saturated with pain? I knew I wouldn't hear his whole story on the front porch of the church.

His wife solved the problem by inviting me to their home for Sunday lunch. I accepted, and thirty minutes later I was sitting at the sergeant's dinner table. After praying over the meal, I asked Bill basic questions about his military career. His answers were brief, as if he were being interrogated rather than involved in a Sunday afternoon lunch with a preacher. I tightened the noose with the following questions:

"What have you enjoyed most in your military career?"

"Not much!"

"What moment in your military career has brought you the most regret?"

If I had hit him in the stomach with a sledgehammer, it couldn't have taken the breath out of him any faster. He stared at me for a full thirty seconds; he put his knife and fork down, as his wife turned pale. His face became flushed with rage, and then tears welled in his eyes. He began to speak about his pain and suffering. I could see emotional barriers coming down as he gushed nonstop for about thirty minutes.

In brief, he had served as the leader of a bomb squad during the Korean War. It was his squad's duty to go into a mine-infested area, find and defuse all the mines, and declare the area *all clear* for the advancing troops.

On one occasion he had personally declared the area *all clear*, and within minutes a soldier stepped on a mine, killing him and several soldiers following him. The soldier who first stepped on the mine was his lifelong friend. They had grown up together as boys and entered the military together, and in an instant his body was blown into pieces.

"My friend and those soldiers are dead because of my failure to find and disarm that bomb. That's my story!" By this time the tears were dripping down his face and onto the table.

"Bill, the only power in heaven or earth that can remove the pain of that horrific experience from your mind and heart is God Himself. Are you willing to forgive yourself and to receive the supernatural comfort of God?" I waited for his answer.

After a long silence he whispered an agonizing "yes!"

"Bill, Jesus made a statement two thousand years ago that applies to you today. He said, 'Blessed are they that mourn: for they shall be comforted.' The promise of comfort echoes again and again through all the Scriptures. 'Comfort ye, comfort ye, My people,' 'Speak ye comfortably to Jerusalem and cry unto her, that her warfare is accomplished.'

Bill, your warfare is over! I am going to ask you to join me in this prayer and receive God's comfort." We joined our hands and prayed together as his tormented soul mourned its way into the peace of God that surpasses all understanding.

Is there something in your past that fills your heart and mind with grief and deep sorrow? Don't allow your past to control your future! Pray this simple prayer and receive the comfort of God:

Almighty and loving Lord, I release the grief and suffering of my past into Your hands. Jesus gave this prophetic proclamation: "Blessed are they that mourn: for they shall be comforted." Father God, I receive Your comfort today and for all my tomorrows. In Jesus' name, Amen!

The Third Prophetic Blessing

Blessed are the meek,
For they shall inherit the earth. (Matthew 5:5)

In a world dedicated to power plays and pushbacks, meekness is not a preferred attribute. Meekness does not appeal to us. We want to be conquerors, and meekness sounds too much like surrender. But meekness does not mean surrendering to those around us or to ourselves. Nor does it mean to surrender to the circumstances of our lives.

The Hebrew word for *meek* really means "to be molded." The true meaning of meekness is revealed in Psalm 37:11: "But the meek shall inherit the earth, and shall delight themselves in the abundance of peace."

Jesus spoke Aramaic. The Greek word used to translate the Aramaic word for *meekness*, which Jesus used in the Prophetic Blessing, was the word used for an animal that had been tamed and brought under the control of the bit and reins of its master. Meekness is power under control!

Self-control—do you have it? You had better find it, because without it, you will destroy yourself. "He who is slow to anger is better than the mighty, and he who rules his spirit than he who takes a city" (Proverbs 16:32).

Self-control is the ability to make yourself do the things you have to do, whether you want to do them or not.

Meekness does not mean you have to let the world run over you. You can stand against injustice and evil with righteous anger and still be meek. Consider Jesus Christ, who said, "Learn of me; for I am meek and lowly in heart" (Matthew 11:29 KJV).

Look at the meek and lowly Son of God enter the temple with whip in hand, His eyes blazing as He shouts at the top of His lungs: "My house shall be called a house of prayer, but you have made it a 'den of thieves'" (Matthew 21:13). Jesus was meek . . . not weak.

I take you back once again to the day of His crucifixion as Roman guards slap His face and mock Him, saying, "Hail, King of the Jews." Look as the spittle from the guards trickles down His face and the blood drips from His brow.

Listen as the Roman cat-o'-nine-tails whistles through the air, ripping His back to shreds of bloody flesh and chunks of bone.

Look toward Calvary as He willingly lies on the cross and lets barbarians drive nails through His holy hands. These are the very same hands that healed the sick and raised the dead. He does not open His mouth—He is meek, not weak.

Why did the Son of God let this happen? Jesus said, "Shall I not drink the cup which My Father has given Me?" (John 18:11).

Jesus had joined God the Father to create heaven and earth in six days. Jesus had commanded winds and waves; He had cast out demons with a word and conquered disease and death as a daily part of His ministry.

He had the power to call ten thousand angels to destroy the earth when He was on the cross. What did He do with all that power? He hung His head and died, giving us the portrait of power under absolute control. He was meek, not weak.

In the book of Matthew, Jesus is the Lamb of God. In Revelation, He is the Lion of the tribe of Judah. He did not open His mouth in Pilate's judgment hall. He was meek, yet

He said to the Pharisees, "You are of your father the devil" (John 8:44). "Serpents, brood of vipers! How can you escape the condemnation of hell?" (Matthew 23:33).

That's power!

Jesus now sits at the right hand of God the Father, which is a position of power. He sees the wicked every day. He sees the murderer and his sobbing victim. He sees the rapist and his screaming prey. He sees the adulterers and their sex partners. He sees the liar, the talebearer, and the gossip sitting in the pews of the house of God—and He holds His fury. He is meek, not weak.

But the day of God's wrath is coming! There will be a payday some day! Don't confuse God's meekness with weakness. Every wrong will be made right on Judgment Day, and every person will give an account of every word, thought, and deed at the judgment seat of Christ.

When Christ returns to earth, He will rule the nations of the world with a rod of iron. Every knee shall bow and every tongue shall confess that "Jesus Christ is Lord to the glory of God the Father" (Philippians 2:10–11). That's power. Jesus Christ is meek, but not weak.

"Blessed are the meek, for they shall inherit the earth." Doesn't that sound absurd? In our hardball society, meekness is not an asset; it's a liability. Haven't you heard the phrase "Good guys finish last"?

Carnal man teaches that the only way to inherit the earth is to be as mean as a junkyard dog: get aggressive, intimidating, and hard-fisted, and do all you must do to win—even run over people.

In America, we frame slogans that inspire us. When did you last see a plaque mounted on a business office wall that said "Blessed are the meek"?

You have seen "Lead, follow, or get out of the way." You have seen "If something you love leaves and does not return, track it down and beat it to death."

Meekness is the opposite of violence!

Americans have rejected meekness as a path to happiness and have inherited a tumultuous philosophy of "take it by force!" What is the theme of the television programming that our children watch as much as forty hours each week? Is it meekness? Is it respect and good manners? Is it morality?

No, it's violence. It's rebellion. It's hate and revenge to the maximum allowed by law. It's the law of the jungle. It's the law of *tooth and claw*. It's the law of *might is right*. It's raw sex, deceitfulness, and corruption. Bottom line, there is a cesspool overflowing from America's television screens and into the hearts and minds of our children.

⅄ THINK ON THIS ⅄

You will become what you behold.

Our rejection of meekness has opened the door to drive-by shootings and to an illegitimate birthrate of nearly 50 percent.[2]

The rejection of meekness fills our courts with mothers and their derelict live-in boyfriends who beat their children to death in fits of rage.

The rejection of meekness sends children to school carrying a gun or knife.

The rejection of meekness has filled the streets of America's cities with gangs that will blow your brains out as part of an initiation ritual.

The rejection of meekness sends mobs of Christmas shoppers who are willing to trample a security officer to death to obtain another electronic gadget for their homes. Can I hear joy to the world?

This open door of no self-control has made way for rape, murder, incest, child abuse, and a crime wave that is overwhelming the police force and flooding our prisons, costing American taxpayers billions of dollars.

Why has this happened in *America the beautiful*? Because we have forgotten the words of Jesus Christ: "Blessed are the meek; blessed are those who live under divine self-control. Blessed are the gentle. Blessed are the disciplined and responsible. Blessed are those who seek after righteousness, for theirs is the kingdom of heaven."

"Blessed are the meek, for they shall inherit the earth." If you will live a life under His control, He will give you the world and all that's in it.

*Seek the L*ORD, *all you meek of the earth,*
Who have upheld His justice.
Seek righteousness, seek humility.
It may be that you will be hidden
*In the day of the L*ORD'*s anger.*
(Zephaniah 2:3)

The Fourth Prophetic Blessing

Blessed are those who hunger and thirst after righteousness,
For they shall be filled. (Matthew 5:6)

In this text, Jesus Christ, the Architect of righteousness, invites you to rediscover your passion.

Jesus said, "Blessed are those who hunger and thirst." How intensely does a starving man seek food? How passionately does a man dying from thirst pursue water? That life-preserving instinct for food and water is the essence of this story.

Jesus was saying through this Prophetic Blessing that the good life comes to the person who pursues righteousness, which is *right living*, as passionately as a starving person pursues food to keep from dying.

It's passion that persuades!

Jesus Christ preached a gospel of passion. He said, "Assuredly, I say to you, there is no one who has left house or brothers or sisters or father or mother or wife or children or lands, for My sake and the gospel's, who shall not receive a hundredfold now in this time—houses and brothers and sisters and mothers and children and lands, with persecutions—and in the age to come, eternal life" (Mark 10:29–30).

That's passion!

Jesus was moved by the four men whose passionate action caused them to find a way to get their paralyzed friend in His presence. When they arrived at the house where Jesus was preaching, the house was packed with those seeking healing (Mark 2:1–12). The friends didn't say, "Too bad, Abe; you're going to die." They ripped the roof off and let him down on a stretcher!

Your problems are not going to be solved until you are willing to do something passionate about them. When conventional methods don't work, try something original: rip the roof off!

When standing at the Red Sea surrounded by adversity, don't just stand there waiting for Pharaoh to capture you and take you back to Egypt. Walk into the water—rip the roof off! Get passionate about reaching the Promised Land! Go from not enough to more than enough!

The athletic team that plays with passion wins. The singer who sings with passion inspires the audience. The businessman who works with passion prospers. A passion to succeed will drive you to overcome every barrier, every resistance, every reversal, and every adversary.

⅋ THINK ON THIS ⅋

If you do not passionately believe it—you will not achieve it!

Jesus said, "Blessed are those who hunger and thirst." Only living things hunger and thirst. Every plant hungers and thirsts, and every animal hungers and thirsts. Every child hungers and thirsts. I have five children, and when they came home from the hospital, they came home hungry! Matthew would lie in his crib, shake his bottle, and if it was empty, throw it against the wall and scream with the passion of a Comanche war cry until relief came.

All of our five children would—without hesitation—wake us up after midnight demanding food. They did not care that their mother and I had just fallen asleep. They did not care that they had single-handedly destroyed our sleep for five nights in a row. They were hungry—and they were hungry *right now*. Those midnight screams were music to my ears.

When they became teenagers and nearly ate us out of house and home, we were thrilled that they were healthy and thriving. It meant that my children were alive, healthy, and growing. When God the Father hears your cry for spiritual food, it's music to His ears. He opens the windows of heaven and pours out the bread of life, the living water, for it is meat for men and milk for spiritual infants.

Because of man's nature, he becomes both hungry and

thirsty; however, he's not always wise enough to seek *good* food. When I was a child, we lived in the country. I was eighteen months old when I crawled behind the kitchen door and found a white square lying on the floor. I tasted it; it was sweet, so I ate it. My mother came in as I was licking my lips and asked, "John, did you eat that?" I gave her the best version of the word *good* I could manage. When she realized what had happened, she grabbed me up off of my feet, ran out the door, and raced toward the hospital. I had eaten rat poison. When we arrived at the hospital, they pumped my stomach to save my life.

Too often we are like children: if something satisfies the instinctual man, we swallow it even if it poisons the soul. We grab at anything that promises satisfaction. We swallow it . . . we smoke it . . . we snort it . . . we shoot it into our veins . . . we view it in porno shops . . . and we watch its toxic poison on computer and television screens—searching for the good life.

Satisfaction will never be found in drugs, alcohol, sexual fantasy, power, or pleasure. Satisfaction is found only in Jesus Christ, the Son of the living God.

What are we to hunger for?

The answer is righteousness! Righteousness is right living; it's life lived by God's standards.

The opposite of righteousness is rebellion. Ignore the righteousness of God, and receive the wrath of God.

Hear the voice of Pharaoh in Egypt: "Who is the Lord that I should obey His voice?" He led his chariots in hot pursuit of the Jewish people at the Red Sea. The towering walls of water that God parted for the Israelites collapsed over Pharaoh and his mighty army. As his bloated body floated to shore, his now sightless eyes could only stare into the face of the God he had rejected. His dazzling signet ring glistened in the sultry Egyptian sunlight as it washed up on the shore. In a matter of seconds, the most powerful man on earth was reduced to fish food.

See pitiful King Saul coming from the cave of the witch of Endor: "God has departed from me and does not answer me anymore, neither by prophets nor by dreams" (1 Samuel 28:15).

America has rejected righteousness. Look at but a few of today's headlines to see what is happening to our children, our families, our schools, our military, our economy, and the very soul of America because we, as a people, have lost our passion for righteousness!

- The traditional family is falling apart; two out of five children in America do not live with their natural fathers.[3]
- Millions of our youth are so addicted to drugs that they cannot function.[4]
- Public schools have become a war zone where the bodies of the dead and the dying lie wounded by the latest crazed shooter.[5]

- Witchcraft is the fastest-growing religion in America.[6]
- Paganism is permitted in the US military.[7]
- America is racing toward financial bankruptcy because our disordered Congress cannot come to grips with debt.
- America is the place where criminals become celebrities, and celebrities do not go to jail.[8]
- America is the place where marriage is being redefined, making the prohibition of a union between two people of the same sex unconstitutional.[9]

Why has this happened in America? Because there is no longer a passion for righteousness in the majority of our country. If you want to experience the good life; it begins with a passion for righteousness. The Bible says, "Righteousness exalts a nation, but sin is a reproach to any people" (Proverbs 14:34). It also says, "Seek first the kingdom of God and His righteousness, and all these things shall be added to you" (Matthew 6:33). God promises the good life to those who diligently seek Him. "He satisfies the longing soul, and fills the hungry soul with goodness" (Psalm 107:9).

The Fifth Prophetic Blessing

Blessed are the merciful,
For they shall obtain mercy. (Matthew 5:7)

Of the eight Prophetic Blessings, mercy is the most appealing and yet the most difficult to apply.

Mercy is appealing because it brings to mind kindness, unselfish service, and goodwill. Everyone loves the Good Samaritan and Florence Nightingale; both lived lives of mercy.

Every person reading this book must realize every day of their lives that without mercy, there is no hope for any of us. The only prayer we can pray is, "God, be merciful to me a sinner" (Luke 18:13).

If you do not extend mercy to another person, God will not extend mercy to you. The most dangerous thing you can do is refuse to show mercy. If you do not repent and forgive others, which in itself is an act of mercy, God says that He will not forgive you. If God does not forgive you of your sins, then eternal life in heaven is impossible. "Therefore be merciful, just as your Father also is merciful. Judge not, and you shall not be judged. Condemn not, and you shall not be condemned. Forgive, and you will be forgiven. Give, and it will be given to you: good measure, pressed down, shaken together, and running over will be put into your bosom. For with the same measure that you use, it will be measured back to you" (Luke 6:36–38).

Being merciful is not just handing out sandwiches and blankets to street people. It's not merely giving to the United Way. Being merciful is more than doing and serving. You can do and serve with a heart of iron. You can do and serve like a machine, a religious robot lacking feeling or emotion.

Mercy is to be a disposition of the soul. Mercy is to be possessed with a forgiving spirit; mercy is to have a heart of compassion. Mercy is to have the mind of Christ toward the suffering and the sinful.

Mercy is to be manifested in the life of the believer. The merciful search for the best in other people. The merciful seek a way to restore the fallen rather than searching for smut in their lives as if it were gold. The merciful are slow to condemn and quick to commend. The merciful empathize: they put themselves in the shoes of other people to see what life feels like from their perspective.

The Bible tells the story of a certain man who went down from Jerusalem to Jericho, fell among thieves who stripped him of his raiment, wounded him, and departed, leaving him half dead. A priest came by and passed on the other side. Likewise, a Levite passed on the other side. These men represented the religious community (Luke 10:30–37).

The truth is that the more religious you are, the more mechanical and less merciful you become. The religious have ceremony without compassion. They have ritual without righteousness. The religious serve denominations—not God. The religious have committee meetings to attend that are more important than souls to save. God is a secondary issue.

Jesus painted a vivid picture of the religious crowd called *Pharisees*: they were cold, calloused, and mean-spirited. They were pompous and legalistic stuffed shirts who couldn't even spell *mercy*, let alone show mercy.

The story continues: "But a certain Samaritan, as he journeyed, came where he [the injured man] was: and when he saw him, he had compassion on him" (Luke 10:33 KJV). He bound up his wounds and poured oil and wine on them; he put him in his pickup truck, took him to the Baptist Hospital, and said, "Here's my American Express card. Take care of this gentleman until I return." That's mercy!

The world remembers the nameless Samaritan centuries later. Why? Not because he was rich, not because he was a genius, not because he was a great physician, but because *he was merciful.* He could not withhold his compassion from someone in need.

Diana and I have a saying that keeps mercy at the forefront of our daily lives: "Put mercy in your Mercy Bank because one day you will need a withdrawal!"

When you can withhold your compassion from someone in need, you have lost touch with God. Not religion—God. You have no mercy!

Christ put the Levite and the priest in the same company as the thieves in this story. Why? Because in an hour of someone's need, they did nothing.

To see evil and not address it is, in itself, evil.

Jesus was mighty, and He was merciful. Mercy drove Him from the balconies of heaven to earth. Mercy drove Him from the presence of God the Father to a manger surrounded by donkeys, sheep, and goats. Mercy drove Him from the princely crown of glory to become a Jewish rabbi, nailed to a cross with spittle and blood running down His face.

Why did Jesus do it? Because He saw you as a slave to sin and Satan! He saw you walking in darkness. He saw you enslaved by misery. He saw the hopelessness in your face and the darkness your future. Mercy drove Jesus Christ to the cross to die in your place.

Stop living a self-centered life! Find someone who needs your help and give it generously. Jesus said, "But whoever loses his life for My sake will find it" (Matthew 16:25). Serving others is the key to the good life. Try it; you'll like it.

> *With the merciful You will show Yourself merciful; with a blameless man You will show Yourself blameless. (2 Sam-uel 22:26)*

> *My mercy I will keep for him forever, and My covenant shall stand firm with him. (Psalm 89:28)*

The Sixth Prophetic Blessing

> *Blessed are the pure in heart,*
> *For they shall see God. (Matthew 5:8)*

What does it mean to be pure in heart?

In the Greek and Hebrew contexts, *pure in heart* means to be single-minded. Single-minded is neither simple-minded nor narrow-minded. Single-minded is to be focused like a laser beam on your purpose in life.

Purity of heart is the will to do one thing. St. Paul said, "One thing I do" (Philippians 3:13). Paul was saying that he was focused on the purpose of his life with laser-beam intensity. If you're going to live the good life, then you must have a pure heart.

St. Paul continued concerning this *one thing*: "Forgetting those things which are behind and reaching forward to those things which are ahead." And later: "Whatever things are true . . . noble . . . just . . . pure . . . lovely . . . of good report . . . meditate on these things" (Philippians 4:8).

People ask the question, "Why am I not successful as a Christian?" The answer is that you have not focused on God's highest purpose for your life. God has a divine assignment for you that no one else can do. You have a high and holy calling. Find it; do that one thing with all of your heart, soul, mind, and body, and you will be living the good life.

Focus on one thing and then do it. Theodore Roosevelt said, "Far better it is to dare mighty things, to win glorious triumphs, even though checkered by failure, than to take rank with those poor spirits who neither enjoy much nor suffer much, because they live "in the gray twilight that knows not victory nor defeat."[10] America now lives in the gray twilight that knows not victory nor defeat. We live in a time when our friends do not trust us and our enemies do not fear us!

It's far better to attempt something great and fail than to

plan to do nothing and succeed. Olympic athletes focus for years like a laser beam on a ten-second dash or a four-minute mile or a two-minute gymnastic routine. For four years, everything they eat and everything they do is focused on that few seconds for absolute perfection. They cross the finish line with tears of joy, because their dedicated focus allowed them to attain their goal.

⅍ THINK ON THIS ⅍

The good life comes when you accomplish your
God-given assignment in life.

The pure in heart have access to God. They are among the most favored in the kingdom of God. Now and in the future, the pure in heart shall see God. Moses saw the Lord in a burning bush and led the Hebrews out of the iron grip of Pharaoh. That moment with God transformed Moses from a simple shepherd to a man with laser-beam passion that crushed paganism in Egypt and set Israel free.

The disciples scattered in terror until they saw the resurrected Son of God. Peter had cursed and denied the Lord. Thomas doubted that Jesus was Messiah. All the disciples returned to their fishing nets, saying, "Forget it—the price of following Jesus Christ is much too great."

Then, when they saw the Lord on the seashore of Galilee, there was an instant and permanent turnaround. Peter preached at Pentecost and three thousand were saved. He walked down the street, and the sick were healed by his shadow. History records that the disciples willingly went to the chopping block, were crucified upside down, cast into prison, and exiled on Patmos; they were sawed asunder and boiled in oil, yet they remained pure in their focus on God's will for their lives.

What changed these men from cowards hiding in shadows to lions of God? The answer is, they saw the resurrected Lord. They touched His wounded side. They ate bread and fish with Him at the Sea of Galilee. Ghosts do not leave crumbs and fish bones on the beach.

The disciples became lions for God because they knew Jesus as the Resurrection and the Life. They were willing to die—but not for a ghost, not for a memory, not for a tomb filled with a dead carpenter. They saw the Lord of glory, the Lamb of God, the Lion of Judah, the Light of the World, and they knew there was an eternal kingdom. They gave their lives for that message and for that kingdom.

When you see the Lord, your burdens will be lifted because He is your burden bearer. When you see the Lord, the darkness of your night will become a brilliant and glorious dawn. When you see the Lord, the chains of misery and the yoke of addiction will be broken.

Since you have purified your souls in obeying the truth through the Spirit in sincere love of the brethren, love one another fervently with a pure heart. (1 Peter 1:22)

The Seventh Prophetic Blessing

Blessed are the peacemakers,
For they shall be called sons of God. (Matthew 5:9)

Peace is precious. An ancient poet once said, "Heap upon other men the treasures of the world, but give me the blessing of peace."

Americans are frantically searching for peace. There are many *things* we desire—health, love, riches, beauty, talent, power—but without peace of mind, all those things bring torment instead of joy. If we have peace, no matter what else we may lack, life is beautiful. Without peace, even a palace of gold is a penitentiary.

Peace is not absolute tranquility. Peace is not detachment from risk and responsibility. Peace is not total security. Peace is not the absence of tension, which is considered the haven of the untroubled life. In this hectic world, there is no such thing as total security or absence of tension. To pray for refuge from risk and responsibility is to pray for the peace of death. There is no peace in withdrawal or retreat from life.

When Jesus said, "Take up the cross, and follow Me" (Mark 10:21), He was telling us to take up our task.

There are giants to defeat, mountains to climb, powers

and principalities to conquer. Christianity is the call to an action-filled life—not a call to a passive death.

Peace is won by accompanying God into the storm. There is peace because He is the Master of the wind and waves. His promise of "Peace, be still" conquers the trials of life.

There is peace in the darkest valley, for David said, "Yea, though I walk through the valley of the shadow of death, I will fear no evil; for You are with me" (Psalm 23:4).

Peace is the gift of God. If we don't fully surrender to Jesus Christ, peace is not possible. The idea of a universal peace for a Christ-rejecting, God-hating, pleasure-loving world enslaved by materialism is an absolute pipe dream. Peace is the gift of God, and He gives it only to those who bow their knee to His Son, Jesus Christ, as Savior and Lord.

There can be no peace of mind until there's peace with God. In every man's heart, there lurks a sense of inner wrongness and a hunger for righteousness. Uneasiness in the heart is the *sense of conviction*, and there is no use sweeping it under the rug or taking it to the seashore or to the mountains of some Shangri-La of forgetfulness. Uneasiness comes from within.

Our generation has dismissed the whole concept of accountability. We have instead chosen to soothe our conscience and excuse our moral irresponsibility.

We have sought to rearrange our attitudes and manipulate our emotions. We have sought for devices that make us feel good without being good. We have tried to banish evil without quitting evil. In the end, we have sought peace of mind without moral price. Simply stated, we want the gifts of God without the need of God.

Adjustment is the new gospel: accept your sins—don't rise above your sins. We seek an alibi for moral failure to reduce the pain of conscience. We feel guilty because we *are* guilty.

⚥ THINK on THIS ⚥

The sense of moral conviction is a divine gift from God.

The last word of our Lord to the church was not the Great Commission. The last word our Lord spoke to the church was *repent*. The message of Revelation 2:5 is "Repent . . . or else."

True peace is a lasting peace. Confess your sin in repentance and be filled with the Holy Spirit. Take responsibility for your life, seek righteousness first, and true peace will come. "Peace I leave with you, My peace I give to you; not as the world gives do I give to you. Let not your heart be troubled, neither let it be afraid" (John 14:27).

The Eighth Prophetic Blessing

Blessed are those who are persecuted for righteousness' sake;
For theirs is the kingdom of heaven. (Matthew 5:10)

Who wants to be persecuted? Who wants to see their name in the headlines of the newspaper or hear it on the television with *breaking news* belching out lies and distortions about what you didn't do and never said? No one enjoys being the object of character assassination. High-tech lynching has become an art form in America's media world.

Why are good people persecuted? Here's a spiritual law that is as unchangeable as the law of gravity: "All who desire to live godly in Christ Jesus will suffer persecution" (2 Timothy 3:12).

From Genesis 1:1 until the end of the age, there has been and will be a vicious battle between the kingdom of light and the kingdom of darkness. America is now engaged in a cultural war that is a clash between good and evil. It is a clash between civilizations. If you are on the side of goodness, evil will target you, slander you, criticize you, and lie about you. It is the nature of a hog to love filth, just as it is the nature of the ungodly to slander and persecute the righteous. Jesus said, "If you were *of* the world, the world would love *its own*. Yet, because you are not of the world . . . the world hates you" (John 15:19).

James wrote, "A friend of the world makes himself an enemy of God" (James 4:4 ESV). In a time of war, you cannot expect the goodwill of the enemy. Satan will command those who follow him to assassinate your character, to slander you, to ridicule you, and to criticize you without cause.

However, you cannot stand on both sides of the battle. Remember the soldier in the Civil War who wore a Rebel jacket and Union trousers—he was shot both in the front and the back! You must choose which side you're on! You are either a servant to Jesus Christ or a slave to Satan! The choice is yours.

Jesus never let the relentless criticism of the Pharisees keep Him from the path of reaching His eternal objective because He knew who He was. He knew who sent Him. He knew His message. He knew He was to die for the sins of the world. He knew His divine purpose. The Bible says, "You shall know the truth, and the truth shall make you free" (John 8:32).

When you realize this truth, you will be free from the fear of criticism. You will be free from those who seek to dominate or manipulate you. You will be free to reach for the greatness God has for you.

What is the New Testament reaction to unjust criticism and slander? God's direct order is "Rejoice and be exceedingly glad" (Matthew 5:12). Laugh! Laugh at your critics. Laugh at the devil. The victory is yours in Jesus' name.

The word *joy* has all but disappeared from Christianity. The world is tired of mule-faced Christians. James said, "Count it all joy when you fall into various trials" (James 1:2). When you are persecuted, remember you are being processed for heaven. No pain—no gain! No cross—no crown. No struggle—no success. No persecution—no great reward.

I have often quoted a giant in world history by the name of Winston Churchill. On May 13, 1940, in his first speech to Parliament after his appointment as prime minister during World War II, Churchill gave a unifying call to his countrymen that relates to all of us who are willing to fight for the spiritual victory without appeasement.

I would say to the House, as I said to those who have joined this government: "I have nothing to offer but blood, toil, tears and sweat."

We have before us an ordeal of the most grievous kind. We have before us many, many long months of struggle and of suffering. You ask, what is our policy? I can say: It is to wage war, by sea, land and air, with all our might and with all the strength that God can give us; to wage war against a monstrous tyranny, never surpassed in the dark, lamentable catalogue of human crime. That is our policy. You ask, what is our aim? I can answer in one word: It is victory, victory at all costs, victory in spite of all terror, victory, however long and hard the road may be; for without victory, there is no survival. Let that be realized; no survival for the British Empire, no survival for all that the British Empire has stood for, no survival for the urge and impulse of the ages, that mankind will move forward towards its goal. But I take up my task with bouyancy and hope. I feel sure that our cause will not be suffered to fail among men. At this time I feel entitled to claim the aid of all, and I say, "come then, let us go forward together with our united strength."[11]

Winston Churchill echoed St. Paul's writings to the persecuted Christians living in Rome: "For your obedience has become known to all. Therefore I am glad on your behalf; but I want you to be wise in what is good, and simple concerning evil. And the God of peace will crush Satan under your feet shortly. The grace of our Lord Jesus Christ be with you. Amen" (Romans 16:19–20).

Christ our Beloved Redeemer foreknew the battles we would encounter, so He imparted eight life-changing Prophetic Blessings to His children. These blessings are the keys to the kingdom of God that guarantee the good life and absolute victory over the world, the flesh, and the devil to everyone who receives them.

My brothers and sisters in Christ, we are in a war for our very spiritual and moral survival. God, our eternal Father has given us a mandate. We are to "seek first the kingdom of God and His righteousness, and all these things shall be added to you" (Matthew 6:33).

SECTION 3:

RELEASING AND RECEIVING THE BLESSING

CHAPTER EIGHT

RELEASING THE PROPHETIC BLESSING THROUGH THE SPOKEN WORD

A bell is no bell till you ring it.
A song is no song till you sing it.
And love in your heart wasn't put there to stay.
Love isn't love . . . till you give it away.[1]

Most of us are familiar with these words written by the incomparable composer and lyricist Oscar Hammerstein. More than just poetic, these words are also very true. Just as "love isn't love till you give it away," so a blessing cannot be a blessing until it is spoken by one in spiritual authority. Of what benefit is it to learn about the power of the Prophetic Blessing if you do not know how to apply it?

THE POWER OF WORDS TO BLESS OR CURSE

Your speech is a gift from God. Man is the only creature to whom God gave the power to communicate through words. Words are a transcript of your mind, a reflection of your heart, and in using them, they paint a picture of your soul. Like most paintings, they can be inspiringly beautiful or downright ugly! Jesus was very aware of what our words reveal, for He said, "Out of the abundance of the heart the mouth speaks" (Matthew 12:34).

Words have the power to bring comfort and healing, or hurt and destruction. The apostle James wrote, "The tongue is a fire, a world of iniquity. . . . and it is set on fire by hell" (James 3:6).

⅋ THINK ON THIS ⅋

The tongue is a boneless creature that is more deadly than a rattlesnake, and lurking behind the enamel fence of your teeth, it is always ready to strike.

The seventeenth-century French church statesman Cardinal Richelieu in *Testament Politique* accurately described the power of words: "Words have destroyed a greater horde than the sword; the wounds inflicted by the sword will soon heal, but the wounds inflicted by the tongue never heal."

How many friendships have been ruined, how many

homes have been wrecked, how many churches have been destroyed, how many divorces have been demanded, how many bloody wars have been started through the power of words?

Toxic words corrupt and defile the mind. There are words of suspicion, words of bitterness, and words of death. Every person reading this book knows someone whose life has been poisoned by the power of words.

The power of life and death are found in the tongue. Jesus was murdered by the words of slanderers before Rome crucified Him on the cross. Solomon wrote in Proverbs 18:21, "Death and life are in the power of the tongue, and those who love it will eat its fruit."

Notice the extreme choices God offers in this verse. *Death* or *life*—nothing in between. There is no middle ground; everything that comes out of your mouth produces hope or despair, a blessing or a curse, life or death. James continued in his epistle: "If anyone among you thinks he is religious, and does not bridle his tongue but deceives his own heart, this one's religion is useless" (James 1:26).

I often hear someone use hurtful words and then end the phrase with "I didn't really mean it" or "I was only kidding!" You may have been joking, but your words were not; they cause pain and insult nonetheless.

A Chasidic tale vividly illustrates the danger of improper speech: A man went about the community telling malicious lies about the rabbi. Later, he realized the wrong he had done, and began to feel remorse. He went to the rabbi and begged his forgiveness, saying he would do anything he could to make amends. The rabbi told the man, "Take a feather pillow, cut it open, and scatter the feathers to the winds." The man thought this was a strange request, but it was a simple enough task, and he did it gladly. When he returned to tell the rabbi that he had done what he requested, the rabbi said, "Now go and gather the feathers."

The man was stunned. "Rabbi, that is an impossible task!"

To which the rabbi responded, "Exactly. You can no more make amends for the damage your words have done than you can collect the feathers that have been carried away by the wind."[2]

⅄ THINK ON THIS ⅄

Words when spoken are like feathers:
they are easily scattered but not so easily gathered.

Speech has also been compared to an arrow: once the words are released, they cannot be recalled, and the harm they do cannot be stopped or predicted. For words—like arrows—often go astray.[3]

Here are a few pearls of wisdom you should file away in your brain bank that will help you lead a successful life:

- It does not require many words to speak the truth.[4]
- Words can make a deeper scar than silence can ever heal.[5]

- Kind words are short to speak, but their echoes are endless.[6]

❦ THINK on THIS ❦

We will all face all of our words on Judgment Day.
The Bible says, "By your words you will be justified, and by
your words you will be condemned" (Matthew 12:37).

THE POWER OF WORDS IN CREATION

The statement "God said . . ." occurs ten times in the first chapter of Genesis, establishing the power of words.

With one statement, God removed the force of darkness over the earth. He said, "Let there be light," and the marvelous and mysterious power of light was born. No one can tell us what light is, only what it does. It is one of the most mysterious elements in the universe. Men have attempted to harness light and, with their effort, have convoluted its purpose, for light has become a new absolute in physics and is the core of $E = mc^2$, a formula that ushered in the atomic age.[7]

God continued to create the universe with the supernatural power of prophetic speech. *"Then God said, '*Let there be a firmament in the midst of the waters, and let it divide the waters from the waters'"* (Genesis 1:6). Through the supernatural power of words, God separated the clouds from the waters of the sea. Not an easy task, my friends, for water is 773 times the weight of air, and there is suspended in the air above the oceans of the world an estimated 54.5 trillion tons of vapor.[8] Finally, a number that is higher than our national debt!

"*Then God said*, 'Let the earth bring forth grass, the herb that yields seed, and the fruit tree that yields fruit according to its kind' . . . and it was so" (Genesis 1:11). Nature in all its splendor was created by the power of God's words. It is important to notice how Moses classified plant life because "botanists use a similar division dividing plants into acotyledons, the seedless plants, monocotyledons, the seed-bearing plants, and dicotyledons, the fruit-bearing plants. This system of classification, the fruit of centuries of research, is still used to this day and was written by Moses in the Bible's very first page."[9]

"*Then God said*, 'Let there be lights in the firmament of the heavens to divide the day from the night; and let them be for signs and seasons, and for days and years; and let them be for lights in the firmament of the heavens to give light on the earth'; and it was so. Then God made two great lights: the greater light to rule the day, and the lesser light to rule the night. He made the stars also" (Genesis 1:14–16).

❧ THINK on THIS ❧

The Bible takes fifty chapters to explain the construction and significance of the tabernacle in the wilderness yet only five words to explain all the stars in the sky. How big are the stars? The star Antares is so large it could swallow up sixty-four million suns the size of ours.[10]

It was nothing for God to create the universe. To create it He had only to speak. However, it was God's silence that made redemption possible as He allowed His Son to be crucified by the created.

WORD AND SPIRIT WORKING TOGETHER

In his book *The Power of Proclamation*, Derek Prince introduced the concept of the written Word of God and the Spirit of God working together to produce the power of the Spoken Word. For instance, when God created man, He said, "Let Us make man in Our [God and Jesus] image, according to Our likeness" (Genesis 1:26). In the next chapter, the Word says, "And the LORD God formed man of the dust of the ground, and breathed into his nostrils the breath of life; and man became a living being" (Genesis 2:7). Again, the Hebrew word for "breath" is *ruach*, meaning "spirit," and with respect to this verse in particular, *ruach* or *breath* is referring to the Spirit of God.[11]

In order to give Adam life, God literally breathed His own Spirit into him. King David spoke of this same creative power when he declared, *"By the word of the LORD the heavens were made, and all the host of them by the breath of His mouth. . . . For He spoke, and it was done; He commanded, and it stood fast* (Psalm 33:6–9).

It is the Word of God that performs the supernatural work, not man, for even Jesus said, *"The Son can do nothing of Himself, unless it is something He sees the Father doing; for whatever the Father does, these things the Son also does in like manner."* We too pass on the Prophetic Blessing when we proclaim it with a believing heart and with believing lips.[12]

⚥ THINK ON THIS ⚥

God is the source and power of His Word; we are simply His vessels that release and receive the Power of the Prophetic Blessing.

THE SUPERNATURAL POWER OF JESUS' SPEECH

When Jesus and His disciples were crossing the Sea of Galilee, the winds became contrary to the point that the disciples—some of whom were professional fishermen—were terrified, thinking they would surely die.

The frightened disciples awakened Jesus, shouting above the howling winds and waves pounding the boat: "'Do You not care that we are perishing?' Then He arose and rebuked the wind, and said to the sea, 'Peace, be still!' And the wind ceased and there was a great calm" (Mark 4:38–39). He spoke . . . and it was so!

Jesus stood before the tomb of Lazarus four days after his death and simply spoke: "'Lazarus, come forth!' And he who had died came out" (John 11:43–44). He spoke . . . and it was so!

Lepers were forced to live outside the city in an isolated colony until death mercifully ended their grueling suffering. However, one leper managed to get to Jesus and make a simple statement: "Lord, if You are willing, You can make me clean." Jesus responded, "I am willing; be cleansed" (Luke 5:12–13). He spoke . . . and it was so!

This voice that calmed the sea, raised the dead, and cured the leper was the same voice that spoke to the darkness on Creation morning, and darkness fled from the face of the earth.

I can read your mind right now. You're saying, "Pastor Hagee, everyone knows the speech of God and that of Jesus, His Son, is supernatural . . . but not mine!" Wrong! Your speech expresses God's power anytime you proclaim the Word of God.

Every time Derek Prince took the pulpit, he spoke about God's Word and its power to heal the sick, deliver the oppressed, and redeem the lost. Derek met His Savior face-to-face several years ago, and I miss him dearly; however, he left with me, and millions of other believers, teachings that are engraved on our hearts for eternity. I will never forget the beautiful word picture he painted when he spoke on the infinite power of God's Word. Allow me to share a portion of his inspirational message with you:

Every Bible-believing Christian has a rod in his hand: the Word of God. Think of your Bible as the only instrument you need in your hand to be able to do everything God calls you to do.

The first thing you need to realize is the power of God's Word. It is a supernatural book. Just like Moses' rod, it contains power. This isn't obvious when you first look at it, but when you understand it, the power is actually limitless.[13]

It is crucial for you to comprehend how powerful your words can be to revolutionize your life, your marriage, your children, and your business, as well as to literally reshape your future.

Whenever the words we say with our mouths agree with the Word of God, Jesus, the High Priest of our confession, will release His authority and His blessing from heaven on our words here on earth (Hebrews 3:1). You have unbelievable supernatural power through your divinely directed speech.

If you refuse to proclaim God's Word over your life and the lives of your loved ones through the Prophetic Blessing, you cut yourself off from your High Priest in heaven. God can only get involved in your life and in your dreams for the future when you call out to Him in prayer. The initiative rests with *you*. The Bible says, "Whatever you bind on earth will be bound in heaven, and whatever you loose on earth will be loosed in heaven" (Matthew 16:19). God is waiting to hear from you before He will release His power to enforce your divine speech.

THE POWER TO SCULPT YOUR FUTURE

The Prophetic Blessing spoken by God's delegated authority has had a profound impact on my life and ministry. We
held a week of services in 1987 when we dedicated Cornerstone Church. My father, Reverend William Bythel Hagee,
spoke into existence the following Prophetic Blessing over
me through his dedication prayer:

> *Our Father, which art in heaven, we come before You to-
> day with our hearts overflowing with gratitude for Your
> faithfulness. "Except the Lord build the house, they labor
> in vain that build it." This house of worship is Your doing,
> and it is precious in our sight.*
>
> *Heavenly Father, accept the work of our hands as
> a sacrifice of praise to Your Holy Name. Let this house
> of prayer be a lighthouse to a world groping in spiritual
> darkness. Let Your Word go forth from this place to the ut-
> termost parts of the earth and let sons and daughters be
> born into the kingdom of God without number.*
>
> *May it be to us and to our children through all the
> coming years a shrine of blessed memories. May it be
> a refuge from the cares and burdens of life. May it be a
> shelter in the times of the storm. Fill this sanctuary with
> Your Holy Spirit and fill us with Your love, peace, and
> joy. As the erection of the temple is in vain without the
> consecration of the people, we offer our lives to You today
> anew as Your servants, Lord. Let Your Word abide in our*

hearts. May we here be changed into Your own glorious image. Let us remember that You are the Cornerstone of this church. You are the precious One. You are the Rock of our salvation.

Our Father, bless those who minister here. May they be vessels fitted for the Master's use. Give them strength for the journey. Anoint their ministry to guide the souls of men in paths of righteousness. When tired, sin-sick, hungry hearts walk through these doors, let them find living water and the bread of life. Hear our prayer, O Lord, our God, our King, and our Redeemer. These things we ask in the Precious Name of our Lord and Savior, Jesus Christ.

Amen.[14]

I am deeply moved every time I read this powerful proclamation over my life. Why? Because it was spoken in faith by God's delegated authority over my life; it was spoken according to God's Word, and I received it and have done what is necessary to see its contents come to pass.

Diana and I attended the International Christian Businessmen's Conference at Oral Roberts University in 1991, held in the Mabee Center. I was serving on the Board of Regents at Oral Roberts University at the time and was also one of the speakers at the conference.

Little did we know that the final plenary session would be a moment in time that would help sculpt our future. As Diana and I sat in the front row with Oral Roberts, the speaker taught from Habakkuk 2:2–3, which states:

Write the vision
And make it plain on tablets,
That he may run who reads it.
For the vision is yet for an appointed time;
But at the end it will speak, and it will not lie.
Though it tarries, wait for it;
Because it will surely come,
It will not tarry.

We listened to the speaker develop the concept of writing down all the things we would like to accomplish in the future. I reached for my Bible, and Diana and I agreed to write down the vision we had for our lives and make a profession of faith that God would bring it to pass. Little did we know that everything we wrote in that Bible on that day would come to pass over the next twenty years exactly as it was written.

Our proclamation for the future:

To build a national television ministry that would reach America and the world for the purpose of preaching all the gospel to all the world.

To build a New Testament church filled with the signs and wonders of the New Testament that would bless the city of San Antonio and America.

To build a Conference Center that would receive the nations of the world to restore, unite, train, and teach the lost, the brokenhearted, and the discouraged, and heal the sick and offer deliverance to the oppressed.

All of this to be done to the glory of God the Father and His Son, Jesus Christ, through the power of the Holy Spirit.

—18 JUNE 1991, ICBM CONFERENCE, ORAL ROBERTS UNIVERSITY

I have this vision statement framed in my office. My life is living proof that the Spoken Word has the power to establish your future when it is in agreement with the Word and the will of God.

Get a vision of what you want God to do with your life, your marriage, your ministry, your business or job, your children and grandchildren. Dare to believe that Jesus Christ is the High Priest of your Prophetic Blessing. Have faith that He will lend His power and authority to fulfill the blessing over your life in agreement with His Word. Live in accordance to your prophetic proclamation and watch God act on your behalf.

Matthew's Story

Diana and I have earned the right to spoil our grandchildren beyond description. My own children know that when their children walk through my door, they walk into the house of *"yes!"*

Yes, you can have ice cream for breakfast. Yes, you can eat chocolate candy before supper. Yes, you can watch cartoons until you fall asleep.

We had great fun raising our five children and are having an amazing time with our twelve grandchildren. We are truly blessed! We are beginning to chronicle stories of our grandchildren, adding to their parents' lists of stories. Allow me to share a little of Matthew's story with you.

When our son Matthew was about nine years of age, he said to his mother as she was tucking him into bed one Saturday night, "I need to talk to Daddy."

My wife has a curiosity factor that runs off the charts. Matt's "I need to talk to Daddy" statement brought a flurry of questions from his mother. "What do you need to talk to Daddy about? Is there a problem? Did you do something wrong? This is Saturday night; you know your daddy is lost in his study for tomorrow's sermon."

Matt stuck by his guns. "Momma, I need to talk to Daddy tonight and I need to do it now!"

Diana came into my study with a very concerned look on her face and repeated Matthew's message. I asked, "What does he want to talk about?"

She responded, "He won't tell me; he said you are the only one he wants to talk to."

I closed my Bible, put my sermon notes in my briefcase, and walked up the stairs toward Matthew's bedroom. My mind was racing as I attempted to envision what had happened in Matthew's young life that made his request to specifically speak to me so urgent.

Of our five children, Matthew was always the most talkative

and articulate. He was practically born talking. He started speaking whole sentences so early in life that adults found it entertaining to hold conversations with him even as a child.

I walked into his room, which was dimly lit by a small night-light beside his bed. I could see tears in his eyes, and my concern factor rocketed off the charts. *What had happened? What had he done?* I was comforted that he was too young to rob banks, take drugs, or chase girls. *What could a nine-year-old boy do to move him to tears?*

I knelt beside his bed as tears ran down his cheeks. I melted like butter.

"What happened, Matt?"

"Daddy," he said with a trembling voice, "I've said something today that I feel has offended God."

"Would you like to talk about it?"

"No! I just want to make sure before I go to bed that God will forgive me, and if you ask Him, I know He will."

As I listened intently, I thought of the prophet Samuel, who as a child heard the voice of the Lord calling him when the high priest of Israel did not hear God's voice. From the moment Matthew was born, Diana and I had prayed the double blessing over his life: "And so it was, when they had crossed over, that Elijah said to Elisha, 'Ask! What may I do for you, before I am taken away from you?' Elisha said, 'Please let a double portion of your spirit be upon me'" (2 Kings 2:9).

In an instant, this bedside chat went from just another talk with Daddy to a moment in time when the hand of God was shaping the future of a child . . . my child. I changed gears from counselor to the high priest of my house.

We asked God for forgiveness, and then I placed both my hands on Matt's head and prayed the Priestly Blessing over my son. Following the blessing, I asked the Lord to protect him from the forces of evil; to forgive him of his offenses; to provide him with good health; and to send angels before him and behind him to guide him all the days of his life.

I asked the Lord to bring Matthew into the service of God as a minister of the gospel and to bring him a godly wife and godly children who would forever be a source of joy in his life. We hugged tightly and I walked out of his room only to bump into Diana, who was sitting at the top of the stairs. I recounted the story, and we held each other and cried, thanking God for our son, for his sensitivity to the Holy Spirit, and for his future.

Twenty-five years later, every word of that Prophetic Blessing has become reality.[15]

Do you want to positively impact the future of your life and the lives of your loved ones? Do you want to renew and reenergize your stagnant marriage? Do you want to breathe hope and prosperity into your business and finances? Do you want to break the yoke of illness in your family? Would you like to have the unlimited favor of God? You have the power to impact your children's and grandchildren's future for good!

Don't wait a moment longer! Begin to pray for each of your children and grandchildren and ask God to reveal to you what you should pray over their lives. Once you have a clear word from the Lord, then lovingly lay hands on them, proclaim the Priestly Blessing followed by the Prophetic Blessing, and watch God begin to work in their lives.

THE SPOKEN WORD IS A WEAPON OF WARFARE

The Bible again paints a picture of the Spoken Word in Ephesians 6 through the teaching on the armor of God:

> *Therefore take up the whole armor of God, that you may be able to withstand in the evil day, and having done all, to stand. . . . And take the helmet of salvation, and the sword of the Spirit, which is the word of God; praying always with all prayer and supplication in the Spirit, being watchful to this end with all perseverance and supplication for all the saints—and for me, that utterance may be given to me, that I may open my mouth boldly to make known the mystery of the gospel, for which I am an ambassador in chains; that in it I may speak boldly, as I ought to speak. (vv. 13, 17–20)*

In this passage the "sword" refers to the actual Word of God (see Revelation 1:16 KJV—"out of His mouth went a sharp two-edged sword"). And the "Spirit" is the *breath* or *ruach* of

God, which I explained earlier in this chapter. So, in commanding us to arm ourselves with "the sword of the Spirit," Paul was not telling us to fight "against the wiles of the devil" by throwing our fourteen-pound Bible at him. No! These verses command us to fight the devil by boldly opening our mouths and literally *speaking* the Word of God.

I cannot say this often enough: Christians must realize that the Spoken Word is an instrument of authority given to us by God to release His power into every area of our lives. The Spoken Word can be used to bless, and it can also be used as a weapon of spiritual warfare against the powers and principalities of darkness. Scripture records the advantage that can be had through the Spoken Word during warfare:

> *Let the saints be joyful in glory;*
> *Let them sing aloud on their beds.*
> *Let the high praises of God be in their mouth,*
> *And a two-edged sword in their hand,*
> *To execute vengeance on the nations,*
> *And punishments on the peoples;*
> *To bind their kings with chains,*
> *And their nobles with fetters of iron;*
> *To execute on them the written judgment—*
> *This honor have all His saints.*
> *Praise the Lord! (Psalm 149:5–9)*

The psalmist is clearly describing spiritual warfare! But more importantly, he is revealing the awesome power that the Spoken Word has over our enemies. The power of the Spoken Word gives the believer the authority to proclaim the promises within the Bible, and one of those promises is victory: "For the LORD your God is the one who goes with you to fight for you against your enemies to give you victory" (Deuteronomy 20:4 NIV). However, unless these promises are spoken, they cannot fulfill their purpose. One must open his or her mouth and proclaim the "judgments written" in order for the power stored within them to be released.

Jesus used the Spoken Word in spiritual battles. In Matthew 4, we read about Satan tempting Jesus. The Holy Spirit led Jesus into the wilderness where, after a forty-day fast, the devil began to tempt Him, saying, "If You are the Son of God, command that these stones become bread" (v. 3). Christ's instant response was, "It is written, 'Man shall not live by bread alone, but by every word that proceeds from the mouth of God'" (v. 4).

In total, Satan tempted Jesus three times, and each time Jesus fought back by opening His mouth and proclaiming the Scriptures.

⅋ THINK ON THIS ⅋

God was the Word and the Word was God, yet even Jesus,
in all of His majesty and power, spoke the Word in a time of
spiritual warfare!

There is no mystery concerning the victor in this fight,
for the Scripture records:

> Jesus said to him, "Away with you, Satan! For it is writ-
> ten, *'You shall worship the Lord your God, and Him only
> you shall serve.'"* Then the devil left Him, and behold,
> angels came and ministered to Him. (Matthew 4:10–11)

Jesus faced spiritual warfare, and so will you. That is guar-
anteed. You can't avoid the battle, but you can be equipped to
win it. God has declared that you have the power to use His
Word as part of your armor to shield you from the enemy's attack. This is a revolutionary thought for many of you. Would
you go into battle without your helmet or bulletproof vest?
Not unless you want to die shortly after the battle begins.

Eva's Story

I heard this powerful testimony from members of our
Cornerstone family. It beautifully illustrates the power of the
Spoken Word in spiritual warfare.

My husband and I were thrilled when we learned that we were expecting our second child. We knew in our hearts that this baby was a little girl long before her sex was confirmed. Our first child was a beautiful boy named Elijah, so we decided to name our little girl Elisha.

I was shocked when the doctor announced at my first visit that the sonogram showed no heartbeat. The doctor said, "I would normally prescribe a D&C, but I'm going to wait two more weeks before I perform the procedure."

Devastated, I went home to my prayer closet for a time of extended prayer. Two weeks passed and I anxiously went back to the doctor, where he joyfully proclaimed that I had a healthy baby growing within me! He announced, "This little one has a purpose!" I knew he was right!

From that moment on I prayed over my unborn baby, calling her by the name we had chosen, Elisha. One morning while I was in my prayer closet, I heard the Lord speak to my spirit, saying, "You shall name this child Eva, for her name means life. There will be many days the enemy will come to speak death, but you will have countered the enemy's efforts every time you speak her name!"

I had no idea what that statement would mean and the power it would hold in the immediate future of our little girl.

When Eva was born, the umbilical cord was wrapped so tightly around her neck that the doctor had to rip the cord in two to ensure her safe delivery.

Still in her infancy, Eva had an unusually allergic reaction that threatened her life. As we rushed her to the hospital, we passionately called out her name and cried, declaring, "The Lord said you shall live and not die!" God miraculously touched our daughter once again.

When Eva was two years of age, she experienced yet another life-threatening crisis. We were out of town and received the terrible call that Eva had accidentally fallen fifteen feet out of a second-story window while under a sitter's care. When I received the horrible news that Eva had split her head from front to back and her bottom lip had detached from her jawbone, my head reeled and my heart sank. Yet I kept proclaiming aloud, "God has promised that she would live and not die!"

As my baby lay in the trauma unit covered in her blood, I stood over her and softly spoke her name. I would say, "Eva, your name means 'life.' Mommy and Daddy declared it from day one, and we believe what God has said is truth!"

We have just celebrated three years since her supernatural recovery from that life-threatening fall. At the age of five, Eva is beautiful, robustly healthy, and full of life. In the many times that Eva's life was in peril, her father and I cried out to God and spoke things that were not as though they were. Every time we called Eva by name . . . we spoke life! We thank God every day that we listened to His voice and obeyed His instruction to name our precious daughter Eva; for God is truly the Giver of life! She is alive today because of the divine power of God's Word.

There is no reason for you, my friend, to lose the battle you are currently fighting; go to the Word. Read it with faith, in faith believe it, in faith declare it, and watch your mountains of impossibility begin to disappear!

Listen and believe the Words of Jesus, " . . . for assuredly, I say to you, if you have faith as a mustard seed, you will say to this mountain, 'Move from here to there,' and it will move; and nothing will be impossible for you" (Matthew 17:20).

THE SPOKEN BLESSING IS PERMANENT

It is important to understand that the Spoken Word is so powerful that once it is proclaimed, it cannot be reversed. I have already discussed that Isaac could not undo the Prophetic Blessing he spoke over Jacob (Genesis 27). God annulled the transgressions of all members of this highly dysfunctional family—including Isaac's preference for Esau, Rebekah's manipulation and dishonesty, Esau's arrogance and selfishness, and Jacob's "heel catching" spirit, which wanted to seize the better blessing. The blessing stayed with Jacob all the days of his life.

In Genesis 12, the Lord spoke the blessing over the children of Israel, saying to Abraham:

I will make you a great nation;
I will bless you
And make your name great;
And you shall be a blessing.

I will bless those who bless you,
And I will curse him who curses you;
And in you all the families of the earth shall be blessed. (vv. 2–3)

The Genesis Blessing could not be revoked. In the book of Numbers, Balaam, who had been sent by the king of Moab to curse the children of Israel, was stopped in his tracks by God Himself. God told Balaam that he would not be able to curse the children of Israel because Balaam could not curse whom God had blessed. Balaam went back to the Moabite king with instructions from the Lord:

Behold, I have received a command to bless;
He has blessed, and I cannot reverse it.
He has not observed iniquity in Jacob,
Nor has He seen wickedness in Israel.
The LORD his God is with him,
And the shout of a King is among them. (Numbers 23:20–21)

The "shout of a King" was among them! In Genesis 12, the children of Israel had been blessed by the Spoken Word of God, and that blessing was permanent. Throughout history, those who have planned destruction for the children of Israel have been struck down, but the children of Israel not only remain—they thrive. They thrive because the blessings of God, once spoken, become reality, never to be revoked.

In order to make the blessings of God a reality in your life and in the lives of your children and grandchildren, you must release the blessings of God through the Spoken Word. He wants to bless you, but you must take action in order to release the blessing and receive the blessing in your life. Scripture reminds us that we must do our part. We cannot receive without asking, we cannot open a door without knocking, we cannot find without seeking. In the same way, we cannot bless without first releasing the blessings according to the Spoken Word of God.

But what does it say? "The word is near you, in your mouth and in your heart" (that is, the word of faith which we preach): that if you confess with your mouth the Lord Jesus and believe in your heart that God has raised Him from the dead, you will be saved. For with the heart one believes unto righteousness, and with the mouth confession is made unto salvation. (Romans 10:8–10)

CHAPTER NINE

RELEASING THE PROPHETIC BLESSING THROUGH TOUCH

He touched me, and made me whole![1]

People often lament that the blessings of God are not evident in their lives. They believe that the Prophetic Blessing established in the Bible is either an inaccessible prize or something that God capriciously imparts based on the recipients' good deeds. Fortunately for us, and through the goodness of our Creator, we *are* able to release His blessings in our lives, positively impacting our marriages and our relationships with our children and grandchildren as well as experiencing the unlimited favor of God. Christ did it; why can't we?

While here on earth, Christ healed and blessed those around Him through the touch of His hands and the power of His prophetic proclamations. We too have the power of touch when linked to God's Spoken Word!

That there is power in human touch is not a new concept, nor is it an exclusively religious one. This seems like a statement one would read in Scripture or sing in a hymnal. The truth is that science has proven that touch, in and of itself, has healing power. As multiple miracles in the Bible have shown that touch has the power to bless and heal, so medical science has proven that touch not only can heal but also has the power to keep you in good mental and emotional health—two of God's greatest blessings.

Dr. Tiffany Field, founder of the Touch Research Institute at the University of Miami School of Medicine, spoke of the restorative power of touch, saying it yields "specific effects, such as reduced pain for those with arthritis, increased peak air flow for those with asthma, and increased natural killer cell activity for the HIV patient."[2]

Furthermore, scientific studies have shown that children may actually die from lack of physical touch. In a study from the early twentieth century, mortality rates of children who lived in institutional facilities, specifically orphanages and foundling homes, were compared to those of children who had been neglected by their parents.[3]

The obvious thought was that in providing their physical needs, the facilities would have a lower mortality rate among their children than would the children whose parents had abandoned them. Astoundingly, the results showed no difference between the mortality rates of neglected children in families and children in orphanages. Although the institutions catered to the children's physical requirements, such as food, clothing, and shelter, "as many children died as survived" this institutionalized care.[4]

More specifically, a study of American orphanages in 1915 found the mortality rate for children younger than the age of two was between 32 percent and 75 percent, with certain hospitals in Baltimore and New York reaching mortality rates of approximately 90 percent and nearly 100 percent, respectively.[5] Yet, despite this study, roughly fifteen years would pass before these disturbing mortality rates would be attributed to the lack of physical touch. The children in these facilities were not touched due to their caretakers' indifference and because societal norms at the time prohibited it. In the late nineteenth and early twentieth centuries, nurturing contact between caretakers and children at these institutions was uncommon, if not forbidden.[6]

However, in the late 1920s, in an attempt to determine the healing effects touch had on pediatric care, those caring for babies in New York's Bellevue Hospital were required to include physical touch in the daily routines of their pediatric patients. Surprisingly, after the hospital incorporated physical nurturing contact into their treatment plans, the mortality rates of the hospitalized children decreased by over 20 percent.[7] Thereafter, physical contact between caregiver and child became the rule rather than the exception. Once this practice was finally integrated into orphanages, the mortality rates of children within these facilities plummeted.[8]

As important as this study was to the scientific discovery of "touch deprivation" versus the positive impact of touch, one could have reached the same conclusion by reading the Word of God: we can see that Christ set a similar example. Matthew 19:13–15 reads:

> Then little children were brought to Him, that He might put His hands on them and pray, but the disciples rebuked them. But Jesus said, "Let the little children come to Me, and do not forbid them; for of such is the kingdom of heaven." And He laid His hands on them, and departed from there.

In their work The Gift of the Blessing, Gary Smalley and John Trent point out that in laying His hands on the children, Jesus was not only trying to teach the crowd a "spiritual lesson," but, in touching them, He was also meeting the actual needs of the children themselves.[9] The authors pointed out that if Christ's objective were solely to teach, He would have merely used the children as an object in His lesson, as was the case in Matthew 18. There, when asked by the disciples, "Who then is greatest in the kingdom of heaven?" Jesus responded by calling a child over to Him, setting that child "in the midst of them," and pointing out that unless one converts and becomes as "little children," that person will not enter the kingdom of heaven (vv. 1–3).

However, in Matthew 19, not only did Christ teach a spiritual lesson, He also met the physical, emotional, and spiritual needs of the children. Christ, in His perfect wisdom, "demonstrated His knowledge of a child's genuine need": He touched them.[10] In addition to meeting their physical needs, in placing His hands on these children, Christ was also reiterating the importance of touch in the Hebrew tradition of releasing the blessing on our children. One need look no further than Genesis 27, and the "lengths to which Jacob and his mother went to have Isaac's hands of blessing laid on Jacob's head,"[11] in order to realize the significance of touch with respect to receiving the divine blessing of God upon that specific life.

Sandy's Story

I remember the life-and-death crisis Diana and I faced with our youngest daughter, Sandy, within hours after her birth. Even though Diana delivered Sandy three and a half weeks before her due date, all seemed perfect at first. She was beautiful and, more importantly, apparently healthy! After holding our new baby daughter for several hours, Diana and I thanked the Lord for His goodness. I kissed them both good-bye and left the hospital to care for the other four children who were waiting at home. Life could not have been better!

As Diana held Sandy, she examined every detail of our new little girl. When the neonatal nurse came to take Sandy back to the nursery, Diana informed her of the purring sound coming from our precious baby every time she took a breath. The nurse made note and wheeled Sandy out of the room. Diana called me to say good night, and we once again prayed a prayer of thanksgiving for the many blessings God had given us.

Several hours passed before Diana was awakened by three specialists who came into her room for a consultation. They stood by her bed and shared their grim prognosis. "We have examined your baby and have found that her lungs are not functioning properly. After initial blood work, we feel she may have an infection in her bloodstream that may be life threatening. We need your permission to do further testing."

Diana was numb. She quickly signed the papers allowing the doctors to perform a myriad of additional tests on our tiny baby. Then Diana called me. I was awakened well after midnight from a deep and peaceful sleep by the clamoring ring of the telephone—never a good sign in the home of a pastor.

Diana began to tearfully relate what the doctors had said. After consoling my wife with the promises of God, we united in prayer for our daughter. I told Diana I would be at the hospital as soon as the sitter came the next day to care for our other children. I never went back to sleep; instead I prayed until daybreak.

I hurried to the hospital early the next morning and found that Diana was not in her room. I rushed to the nurses' station and they directed me to the neonatal unit, where I found Diana's swollen eyes staring into a plastic container that held our baby. The last time I had seen Sandy, she was in her mother's arms, swaddled in a pink blanket with her radiant, thick, black hair showing under her pink stocking cap. Now she was attached to what seemed like every wire imaginable connected to a battery of monitors. Her little chest heaved up and down as she struggled for every breath. I looked into Diana's eyes and saw a distraught mother watching her baby fight for her life. Tears streamed down my face. I held my wife and whispered, "Lord, God of Abraham, Isaac, and Jacob, help us!"

We sat together staring at our precious gift of life, feeling helpless. Suddenly a nurse approached us and said, "Don't be afraid to touch your baby. Please make sure you are sanitized, and then you can place your hands in the incubator and let her know you are here." Diana and I were both relieved that we could show our new baby that we were there for her.

We both washed our hands thoroughly and donned special sterilized gowns, gloves, caps, and shoe covers. I approached the plastic container that was holding our treasure. The nurse opened the incubator door, and I remember placing my massive hand on her tiny, heaving chest, fearing I could somehow harm her. I cried out, "Lord, I ask that You heal my baby. Give her the fighting spirit to overcome this battle. I choose life over death and blessings for her life now and forevermore. Father, direct earthly physicians and bring healing to our baby."

From that moment, we never left Sandy's side. Diana and I touched her little body at every given opportunity. We sang to her, told her we loved her, and prayed for her without ceasing. In fact, Diana's obstetrician wanted to release her on the third day after Sandy's birth. Diana passionately refused to leave the hospital, stating, "I am not leaving this hospital without my baby!" The wise doctor changed his mind.

Our baby Sandy's little body endured six straight days of invasive testing. On the seventh day the doctors met with us once again to present their findings. I sat next to Diana and tightly held her hand as the doctors walked into our room, taking their seats in front of Diana's bed. Our hearts pounded as we waited to hear their results. The head neonatologist took away our breath with his first words: "We don't know quite how to tell you, but . . ." He paused for what seemed an eternity.

"Shortly after your baby's birth, she developed breathing problems as well as an infection in her blood. However, after thoroughly testing your baby, we find that she no longer shows any signs of either problem. I don't believe we made an initial misdiagnosis, but all we can say is that she is healthy and ready to go home."

"Healthy and ready to go home!" That is what we heard—it was music from heaven. Diana already had her bag packed. We could not leave the hospital quickly enough. We were so thankful to God for hearing our prayer and healing Sandy. We waited for the nurse to bring her to us—and realized it was the same nurse who had given us permission to touch Sandy when she was battling for her little life. We thanked the nurse profusely for her encouragement.

She shared our excitement about our good news and explained that she had cared for babies born with minor problems who had no one to love them or touch them, and that for no medical reason they just slowly gave up their will to live and died. She informed us that the hospital had initiated a grandparent program where older volunteers would come and hold sick little babies and love them until they were out of danger. The power of a loving touch has the power of life!

The power of the Prophetic Blessing also endures. I had prayed that Sandy be given a "fighting spirit" to win her battle, and that spoken blessing stands to this day. Sandy is now an attorney who uses that fighting spirit in her daily life. She has also had to call on that supernatural inner strength several times in the lives of her own children. The power of the spoken blessing prevails and overcomes!

The need for touch is not just a childlike trait, nor is it something we ever outgrow. Science has confirmed that whether you are an unborn child in your mother's womb or a centenarian in the latter years of life, your physical need for touch never ceases. The truth is, as you become older, your need for human touch increases. While researching the scientific evidence with respect to the power of touch, I came across some facts that resonated with me on a personal level.

In her book *Touch*, Tiffany Field has pointed out that the older people get, the more they want to be touched. But ironically, the older someone gets, the less opportunity there is to be touched by another. Whether it is due to losing a spouse, friends, or family to death or failing health, there are myriad reasons why one's increasing age leads to a decrease in the type of social exchanges that foster human touch and interaction.[12] In fact, research has shown that "sensory deficits" lead to a surplus of "senile traits" in elderly nursing home residents.[13] Conversely, those residents who received touch in the form of massage therapy, hugs, or even a simple squeeze to the arm displayed fewer senile traits.

Vada's Story

These truths hit particularly close to home for me. For years, I begged my widowed mother to move from her home in Channelview, Texas—where she lived with my father for most of their married life—to San Antonio, where I have lived for more than fifty years.

Despite my repeated requests for her to move to San Antonio, Mother refused to leave her home. Obligingly, I honored her wishes and made the most of the visits she and I had together. My mother was extremely independent. She continued to run the family business after my father died, and she was very successful. She was not concerned about living alone. In fact, Mother was a lover of her Second Amendment rights and was not afraid to use them. My brother and I had to remove the firing pin from the loaded gun she kept under her pillow for fear she would hurt herself or some unsuspecting visitor.

But, from one visit to the next, I noticed a difference in my mother. While her body was sound and her health intact, there was a change in her. I did not know the source of the problem, but I knew something was amiss. After twenty years of obeying her desire to stay in her home alone, I realized that I would have to act against the wishes of my very strong-willed mother and bring her to my hometown. She had reached the mental state where she did not know whether she had eaten or not; she left the gas on the stove wide open without lighting the flame; and eventually she did not recognize her own children when they walked into the room.

Upon my mother's arrival in San Antonio, Diana and I met with the best doctors available in order to find what was wrong with her. Was it Alzheimer's or dementia? Extensive medical evaluations determined that my mother was physically sound although very frail. Her heart was strong; her lungs were clear; and despite some common ancillary health issues, which most people encounter at ninety-two years of age, there was nothing wrong with her physical health per se.

So, what was the problem? In laymen's terms, the doctors said that the lack of sufficient daily interaction with other people due to her living alone for so many years had a deteriorating effect on her mind. She had a mild degree of dementia due to a simple lack of human contact.

I was extremely frustrated with myself for not making my mother move earlier. Because of her partial immobility, we found a superb facility less than a mile from my office so that I could visit her regularly. In addition to the aides at the care center, Diana hired wonderful caretakers to be with my mom twenty-four hours a day. We knew the facility was adequately staffed and had the finest nurses and doctors in the city, but we did not want my mother to face another moment alone.

Not only did I not want her to *be* alone and have any of her needs go unnoticed—I did not want her to *feel* alone. There are subtleties that are easy to miss when you have to care for multiple people, such as a sigh that may signal a need or a moan that might indicate discomfort. No matter what happened, someone was always there to reassure Mother that she was not alone.

In addition to helping with her prescribed medical care, my mother's caregivers—whom we referred to as her "little angels"—also held her hand, patted her face, and massaged her body with soothing lotion from head to toe twice each day. They spoke to her lovingly and often, even when she did not respond verbally. Astoundingly, we began to realize that my mother's caregivers, initially hired to provide nothing more than companionship and our peace of mind, kept her "in touch" with life through their constant and loving interaction with her. When she moved to San Antonio, she was a gaunt reflection of her former self; within months her weight became once again "Hagee healthy." More so, many of the symptoms of dementia disappeared.

Three different times after my mother had strokes and double pulmonary embolisms, the doctors told me to say good-bye to her because she could not possibly live through the night. I spent those nights beside Mother's bed, holding her hand, kissing her cheek, and singing softly the songs of the church she had taught me as a child.

On one of those occasions, the doctors said, "This is her last night." As I watched a battery of nurses come in and out of her room in an attempt to make her last moments comfortable, I waited for angels to escort Mother into her eternal home. I waited, but they didn't show up!

As morning broke with the sunlight beaming into her room and falling softly on her face, she awakened, looked right at me with her piercing eyes, and asked in her General George Patton manner, "What are you doing here?"

"I thought you might need some company!" I responded in amazement. Her doctor had previously informed me that, due to a massive stroke, she could not swallow or speak. You can imagine my thrill when I heard her ask, "Where is my coffee?"

Mom always began her day with a cup of hot coffee and a piece of buttered toast. Then after lunch she would drink her second cup of coffee with a slice of cake or a piece of pie. On this particular morning Mother went *all in* with the command "Bring me a cookie, please!"

I did as I was told!

She soaked the cookie in her coffee and consumed both. Her doctor walked in as she finished her breakfast, and I greeted him with these words: "The corpse is eating, drinking, and talking this morning. Her blood pressure, according to those machines, is better than mine. Cancel hospice care; Vada is alive and well!"

My mother desired to go to heaven more than my grandchildren want to go to Disney World, yet she graduated from hospice care three times in her last four years! The Lord had many opportunities to call my mother home. Mother made it known decades ago that she did not want us to ever prolong her life artificially, and we honored her wishes. When difficult choices needed to be made, we simply chose life as we prayed for her. The Word of God clearly instructs, "I have set before you life and death, blessing and cursing; therefore choose life, that both you and your descendants may live" (Deuteronomy 30:19). And in every case God intervened and kept His Word as she amazed her doctors and defied the odds.

I admit, I did not expect my mother to almost become a centenarian, and I often wondered what the Lord planned for her life. However, I am convinced that the *power of a loving touch* assisted in extending my mother's life.

I know God is too wise to make a mistake, and He is too loving to be unkind. I thank the Lord for the extra time He allowed me to have with my mother, and I know that if nothing else, she was my number-one prayer warrior. For that, I will be eternally grateful and forever indebted to my mother who, through the power of parental blessing, changed my life forever.

When I was a child, Mother would gather her sons for prayer every night, but Saturday night was always in preparation for church on Sunday, where the Hagee family spent the entire day. Our Saturday night ritual was to listen to the Grand Ole Opry on the radio as we ate freshly made popcorn and drank sweet tea out of quart jars.

As the evening would come to a close, we'd gather for prayer in our living room, then Mom would place her hands on the heads of her children and pray the Prophetic Blessing of God into our lives. I can still hear my mother's fervent prayers—she never doubted the power of the Spoken Word of God. As a child, I almost felt sorry for the devil when I heard this zealous prayer warrior in action. I was confident that he was trembling in the corners of hell, for Vada Hagee had a very personal relationship with Jesus Christ.

A loving and merciful God has certainly heard and

answered her prayers all these many years. I am confident that without the Prophetic Blessings spoken over me by my mother, my life would look very different today—and not in a good way. I am so thankful that I was raised in a godly home and that through her obedience to God, my mother fulfilled her role as spiritual authority over her children, blessing our lives in countless ways.

Thirty days short of her ninety-ninth birthday—on April 30, 2012—my mother and the Lord made final earthly arrangements. God sent His heavenly hosts to escort Vada Mildred Hagee through the gates of heaven into her glorious eternal home where she had longed to be for so many years. As she left the bondage of her frail earthly tent, her spirit proclaimed, "I have fought the good fight, I have finished the race, I have kept the faith" (2 Timothy 4:7). And with that, she entered heaven, leaving me and those who follow behind me with this mandate: "Be watchful in all things, endure afflictions, do the work of an evangelist, fulfill your ministry" (v. 5). I love you, Momma.

THE HIGH PRIEST OF YOUR HOME

Just as my mother had authority over her children, so my father had authority over our household. In fact, there is a parallel relationship between Christ as the head of the church and the father as the head of the Christian home.

Jesus Christ is our High Priest. Just as the Levitical high

priests of the Old Testament were the conduits between the children of Israel and God Almighty, so Jesus Christ came to earth to serve as our lifeline to the Father. Hebrews reads, "Seeing then that we have a great High Priest who has passed through the heavens, Jesus the Son of God . . ." (4:14).

Moreover, just as Jesus is the High Priest of His church, so fathers are the high priests of their households (Ephesians 5:23). Just as Christ laid His hands on earthly children, so should a father lovingly lay hands upon his children in order to release the power of the Prophetic Blessing into their lives.

In the book of Numbers, the Lord gave specific instructions with respect to blessing the children of Israel. He instructed Moses to have Aaron, their high priest, bless the children of Israel by reciting the Priestly Blessing:

> *The Lord bless you and keep you;*
> *The Lord make His face shine upon you,*
> *And be gracious to you;*
> *The Lord lift up His countenance upon you,*
> *And give you peace. (Numbers 6:23–26)*

Then, in verse 27, the Lord continued: "So they shall put My name on the children of Israel, and I will bless them." In practice, not only did the priests bless the children of Israel by saying the name of God, but they literally took their fingers and traced the name of God upon the foreheads or right hands of whomever they were blessing. In doing so, the priests were physically touching and putting God's name upon the children of Israel.[14]

This form of touching is so crucial that from the time of Moses until today, every Friday at sundown in Jewish homes around the world, fathers put their hands upon their children's heads and bless them with these very same words. While the Jewish people are the physical descendants of Abraham, Christians are his spiritual descendants. Galatians 3:29 says, "And if you are Christ's, then you are Abraham's seed, and heirs according to the promise." Therefore, Christian parents—as Abraham's seed—should place their hands upon their children and bless them as well.

Not only are parents to use touch to bless their children, they should also use touch to train their children. In Ephesians, the Word says, "And, ye fathers, provoke not your children to wrath: but bring them up in the nurture and admonition of the Lord" (6:4 KJV). While we are all familiar with the biblical mandate to discipline our children, I fear some may overlook the mandate to "bring up" their children. The Greek translation of the words *bring up* is *ektrepho*, which means, as indicated in the King James Version, "to nourish up to maturity" and "to nurture."[15]

Colossians 3:21 commands fathers not to "provoke your children, lest they become discouraged." Accordingly, nurturing requires more than simply providing what is physically required for survival. To nurture one's children is to hug them, hold them in your arms, speak lovingly to them, encourage them, and kiss them on a daily basis. Most importantly, whether you are disciplining your children or nurturing them, all of these acts should be carried out in love. After all is said and done, more is usually said than done. Love is not what you say; love is what you *do*! What better way to show that you love your children than through tender, loving touch?

Unfortunately, not only do some parents neglect to bless their children with words; they also fail to touch them in meaningful ways. Notice again in the aforementioned scripture from Ephesians that fathers are to "bring" or "nourish" their children "up to maturity." The point is that parents need to nourish their children in these meaningful ways until they are grown; ideally until they find a spouse, who then assumes the role of nurturer. So imperative is touch to the ongoing development of a child into an adult that research suggests physical violence in adolescence is the result of childhood touch deprivation.[16]

A study conducted by Dr. J. H. Prescott "reported that most juvenile delinquents and criminals come from neglectful or abusive parents" and that "the deprivation of body touch, contact and movement are the basic causes of a number of emotional disturbances."[17] Central to Dr. Prescott's theory is that "lack of sensory stimulation in childhood leads to addiction to sensory stimulation in adulthood, resulting in delinquency, drug use and crime."[18]

This study was conducted in forty-nine comparable nonindustrial cultures around the globe. The only distinguishable differences in these otherwise similar cultures were that when children within a particular culture received minimal physical affection, that culture displayed high rates of adult violence.

Conversely, when a culture displayed high levels of physical affection toward their children, there was no adult violence present.[19] Dr. Prescott's study appears to be the Word of God on display and is an almost exact example of what happens in a culture when fathers provoke their children to wrath. It never ceases to amaze me when I see the truth of Scripture proven absolutely true in the crucible called life.

Despite the fact that touch has been shown to be a necessary component of healthy development, in America's overly litigious society meaningful touch is practically prohibited. A study conducted at the Touch Research Institute Nursery School found that, in spite of the school's name, its staff rarely touched its students. Fear of being accused of sexual abuse was the teachers' motivation in refraining from touching their students.[20]

How ironic that in today's "enlightened" society, we have become so disoriented about what is appropriate for children. So much so that some people have called for sex education to begin in kindergarten, yet our educators are afraid to give their students a reassuring pat on the back lest it be misinterpreted as sexual harassment.

Isn't it just like the enemy to take something that God has

given us—such as the power of touch—and try to use it as a weapon against us? So, do not let the secular progressives take from us what God has blessed us with—the power of touch! God has blessed us in order that we may be a blessing. God has given us a mandate to lovingly touch others, and evidence of this is seen throughout the written Word: from God's creation of Adam and Eve in the Garden (Geneis 2:7) to the command Christ gave to His church to touch (*"they will lay hands* on the sick, and they will recover" [Mark 16:18]). As believers, we must touch in order to bless. Without loving touch, we are missing the mark in releasing the power of God's blessings upon our children, and our grandchildren, and for future generations.

HUG SOMEBODY!

Have you ever hugged someone who then stiffened up or seemed uncomfortable? More than likely, that person has not experienced a truly loving touch in his or her life. I am a hugger; hugging is my way of encouraging others. What's so good about a hug? Hugging is healthy—it helps the body's immune system. It cures depression, reduces stress, induces sleep, is invigorating, is rejuvenating, and has no unpleasant side effects. Hugging is nothing less than a miracle drug.

As my daughter-in-law Kendal, who is a nurse, constantly tells us, "Hugging releases endorphins, and endorphins make you feel good!" In fact, she said that the ICU nurses witnessed their patients' heart rates decrease to normal readings and their tense muscles relax when they were hugged or gently massaged by their caregivers during their recuperation.

Hugging is all-natural. It is organic and naturally sweet; it has no pesticides, preservatives, or artificial ingredients; and it is 100 percent wholesome. Hugging is practically perfect. There are no movable parts, no batteries to wear out, and no periodic checkups. It has a low-energy consumption, a high-energy yield, no monthly payments, and no insurance requirements. It is inflation-proof, nonfattening, theft-proof, nontaxable, nonpolluting, and, of course, fully returnable. "Happy hugs" are priceless, yet they cost nothing—what more can you ask for?

Hugging is no doubt one of the most naturally therapeutic actions in which we can engage. It seems to me we owe it to ourselves and to those we love to frequently share this mutually beneficial gift.[21]

If you can hug your children and grandchildren, then you can bless them! When is the last time you lovingly placed your hands on those you love and blessed them?

Don't think about it . . . *do it!*

Chapter Ten

RECEIVING THE PROPHETIC BLESSING

Therefore I say to you, whatever things you ask when you pray,
believe that you receive them, and you will have them.

—Mark 11:24

God enters by a private door into the soul of every man. When a person takes one step toward God, the Almighty takes a giant leap toward that individual to forever embrace that person as one of His own.

Receiving the Prophetic Blessing is a step man takes toward God; it is driven by the soul's thirst for more of the Divine: "As the deer pants for the water brooks, so pants my soul for You, O God" (Psalm 42:1).

Throughout history, though, countless blessings have been lost. A lost blessing is a blessing that has not been released by spiritual authority or a blessing that has not been received by the person over whom the blessing was spoken.

Sadly, I have seen many people lose their divine direction in life because their fathers or mothers have refused to speak the blessing over them. I have also seen godly and faithful parents speak the blessing over their offspring but the wayward child refused to accept the blessings spoken over his or her life.

Even more sadly, I have also met people who don't feel that they qualify for the Prophetic Blessing. As a pastor, I grieve over those in my flock who miss out on what God has planned for their lives because they believe they are unworthy. Remember: you were born to be blessed!

And I have more good news! A High Priest by the name of Jesus Christ has declared that every blessing recorded in Scripture is available to you for the asking. You have not because you ask not. Ask NOW and receive the blessing that God the Father ordained specifically for you since the beginning of time.

RECEIVING THE BLESSING THROUGH FAITH

Throughout Scripture, God presents Himself to man through propositional revelation. Put simply, God declares to man: "If you will . . . then I will . . .":

If you *will indeed obey My voice and keep My covenant,* then you *shall be a special treasure to Me above all people; for all the earth is Mine. (Exodus 19:5)*

Now it shall come to pass, if you *diligently obey the voice of the* LORD *your God, to observe carefully all His commandments which I command you today, that* the LORD your God will *set you high above all nations of the earth. (Deuteronomy 28:1)*

If My people, *who are called by My name, will humble themselves, and pray and seek my face, and turn from their wicked ways,* then I will hear *from heaven, and will forgive their sin and will heal their land. (2 Chronicles 7:14)*

If you *forgive men their trespasses,* your heavenly Father *will also forgive you. (Matthew 6:14)*

Through these promises, God is revealing to believers that when they act, He will *then* release His many blessings through acceptance, answered prayer, and total forgiveness.

THE PRICELESS TREASURE

The blessing is God's priceless treasure. Throughout God's Word His blessings are passed from person to person and generation to generation. For instance, the same blessing that Aaron spoke over the children of Israel in Numbers 6 is the same blessing Jewish fathers all over the world pray over their families today.

I was visiting with Rabbi Aryeh Scheinberg about this very subject, and I was deeply moved when he said, "Every Friday evening of my life I have either received the blessing or I have released the blessing."

Blessings in Scripture come alive when they are released through the prophetic proclamation of God's delegated authority and accepted in faith by the recipient. Do you want to receive the blessings of God? In order to receive God's many blessings, which are proclaimed in His Word, you must first qualify for the blessing by accepting the High Priest named Jesus into your life.

The most priceless blessing of God the Father is our redemption through Jesus Christ, His Son and our Savior. I always tell my congregation that if you cannot remember the moment when you accepted Christ as Savior, then you should reexamine your experience. Your salvation should be personal, specific, and life changing.

On the second Thursday of January 1958, I was sitting in the back pew of my father's church in Houston, Texas. Coming to Christ and becoming involved with the church in any way was *not* on my bucket list—yet on this particular day I wanted Christ in my life more than I wanted air to breathe. My mother's prayers were finally answered when I walked up the aisle of the church and received Jesus as my Lord and Savior.

If you cannot remember your life-changing moment, I encourage you to pray this simple yet profoundly transforming prayer now:

Lord Jesus Christ, I come to You this day and I ask that You forgive me of my sins and come into my life as my Lord and Savior. Amen.

When you pray this simple prayer, Christ affords you eternal life! He has forgiven you of even the vilest of transgressions. He has redeemed you from sickness, poverty, strife, and the kingdom of darkness. The prayer of salvation opens the door to the unlimited blessings of God and the good life that lasts forever.

The second requirement is believing *in faith* that just as Christ through this simple prayer saved your soul, your faith and obedience to God's Word will then cause His blessing to be released in your life.

Faith is a gift from God, and salvation through Jesus Christ is ours through faith (Ephesians 2:8). The Bible says, "Without faith it is impossible to please Him, for he who comes to God must believe that He is, and that He is a rewarder of those who diligently seek Him" (Hebrews 11:6).

☩ THINK on THIS ☩

If you can believe it, you can receive it!

BELIEVE IN ORDER TO RECEIVE

The Bible tells us, "Faith is the substance of things hoped for, the evidence of things not seen" (Hebrews 11:1). Many people have faith in God, but there is a difference between having faith in God and believing that He *can* do it versus having faith in God and believing that He *will do it* for you. In Mark 9:23, Jesus said, "All things *are* possible to him who believes."

Do not let the enemy tell you that you do not have faith. The Word tells us that God has given everyone in the body of Christ "a measure of faith" (Romans 12:3). Therefore, knowing that God has given you a measure of faith, it is your responsibility to remove all doubt from the equation and leave room for nothing but faith in your walk with God. When teaching His disciples about faith, Jesus said to them:

> *Have faith in God. For assuredly, I say to you, whoever says to this mountain, "Be removed and be cast into the sea," and does not doubt in his heart, but believes that those things he says will be done, he will have whatever he says. Therefore I say to you, whatever things you ask when you pray, believe that you receive them, and you will have them. (Mark 11:22–24)*

In this passage, Christ has revealed the steps to receive the blessing:

1. Do not doubt in your heart.
2. Believe it will be done.
3. Ask for it.
4. Receive it.

But above all, we must believe. We have all heard the common phrase "I'll believe it when I see it." Although it's catchy, this phrase describes a mentality that has no place in your Christian walk. With respect to your faith, believing comes before seeing.

Therefore, just as God Himself called those things that are not as though they were (Romans 4:17), so should we believe the same. Case in point, Abraham was childless and old when God promised him that he would be the father of many nations. Despite his circumstances, Abraham believed the Lord, and the Lord counted him righteous for it (Genesis 15:6).

The Word says that despite his old age, Abraham "against hope believed in hope, that he might become the father of many nations. . . . And being fully persuaded that, what [God] had promised, he was able also to perform" (Romans 4:18, 21 KJV).

Abraham became Isaac's father because he believed that God would act on His promise; he was strong in his faith (Romans 4:20). Likewise, you must believe that God will fulfill

His promises to you no matter the circumstance. The promises of God have been set before us in His Word, but unless we exercise the righteousness of our faith, we do not have access to those promises (Romans 4:13).

THOUGH IT TARRIES . . . IT WILL SURELY COME

Although God counted Abraham righteous because of his faith, Abraham's faith was still tested. While Abraham received and believed the promise of God for a son, he still had to wait decades to see it fulfilled.

Do not think that the testing of your faith is a result of your lack of faith (James 1:3–4). The enemy would love for you to believe nothing more. So many times people pray in faith believing, and when they do not soon receive what they are seeking, they begin to question their faith.

So, when God has given you a promise, and in faith you receive that promise, even though it may not immediately happen, the Word tells us "Though it tarries, wait for it; because it will surely come." Remember: "The just shall live by his faith" (Habakkuk 2:3–4). So if you are waiting and you feel like your blessings tarry, just wait a bit longer. "Wait on the LORD; be of good courage, and He shall strengthen your heart; wait, I say, on the LORD!" (Psalm 27:14).

⅄ THINK ON THIS ⅄

God's delays are not His denials.

IN HIS OWN TIME

God will do things according to *His own time* and in *His own way*. In the book of Isaiah, the Lord speaks these words: "'For My thoughts are not your thoughts, nor are your ways My ways,' says the LORD. 'For as the heavens are higher than the earth, so are My ways higher than your ways, and My thoughts than your thoughts'" (55:8–9).

The children of Israel left Egypt in a day but it took forty years to get Egypt's unbelief out of them. Pharaoh was not about to let his national labor force escape from Egypt. God hardened Pharaoh's heart, and with six hundred Egyptian chariots, the Pharaoh pursued the children of Israel.

Despite the miracles of the ten plagues that the Hebrews had already witnessed, they were terrified when they saw the Egyptian chariots coming after them (Exodus 14:19–10).

However Moses, believing in God's promise and knowing that His ways are not our ways, turned to the Israelites and said: "Do not be afraid. Stand still, and see the salvation of the LORD, which He will accomplish for you today. For the Egyptians whom you see today, you shall see again no more forever. The LORD will fight for you, and you shall hold your peace" (Exodus 14:13–14).

God chose to give the children of Israel eternal victory over their enemies once and for all. In doing so, the Almighty gained "honor over Pharaoh and over all his army," so that the Egyptians would know that He is the Lord (Exodus 14:4).

If a spiritual authority has spoken a Prophetic Blessing over your life based on God's Word, and you have received it in faith believing, do not be afraid if you turn around one day and see trouble chasing you. Stand still and see the salvation of the Lord.

Be confident that He will accomplish what He said He would accomplish.

⚥ THINK on THIS ⚥

The trouble that you see today you shall see no more.

Have peace and know that the Lord will fight for you. The Lord's ways are not our ways, but in the end, He will bless you in such a manner that only He can get the glory, for all will know that it is the Lord who blesses you.

FAITH IN ACTION

Indeed, faith is so powerful it has the ability to change the mind of God. In her writings, Dr. Lilian B. Yeomans discussed how Hezekiah did just this.[1] She recounted Isaiah 38, which tells us: "In those days was Hezekiah sick unto death. And Isaiah the prophet the son of Amoz came unto him, and said unto him, Thus saith the LORD, set thine house in order: for thou shalt die, and not live" (v. 1 KJV).

What would you do if the Creator of life proclaimed your demise? Can you imagine hearing a death sentence so certain? Most people would begin writing their last will and testaments and dictating their own obituaries if God Himself had said they were to die—but not Hezekiah.

The next verse says that Hezekiah "turned his face toward the wall, and prayed unto the LORD" (Isaiah 38:2 KJV). Dr. Yeomans wrote that, in turning his face to the wall, Hezekiah was turning away "from man, even from Isaiah, the greatest of the prophets; away from his own sensations, symptoms, and sufferings; away from sympathizing friends and relatives . . . and saw nothing but God."[2]

Hezekiah was not ready to die. In faith, he prayed to the Lord, and God answered him. God was so impressed with Hezekiah's faith to believe that nothing was impossible, that He blessed Hezekiah with fifteen additional years of life. Dr. Yeomans summed it up succinctly: "He [God] has made man's faith a determining factor in the execution of divine purposes and the indispensable prerequisite to being so used is that we turn our faces to the wall and see nothing but God."[3]

Dr. Yeomans teaches us an important lesson: we cannot allow the circumstances that surround us to influence our faith. The Bible tells us to walk by faith, not by sight (2 Corinthians 5:7).

Hezekiah was a dead man walking, but instead of focusing on his demise, he turned his face away from what he heard and chose to focus on nothing but God. So, the next time your circumstances do not match up with your expectations, don't focus on the calamity of the moment, but instead turn your face to the wall—away from the world—and see nothing but God.

In Luke 17, Jesus could see the faith of the leprous men who had come out to meet Him. But upon seeing their faith, He did not heal them instantly; instead He told them to go show themselves to the priests, who would have been the final judge of whether or not the men were sufficiently cleansed and could re-enter into society. In commanding them to visit the priests, Christ was asking them to put their faith into action. As a result, verse 14 says they were healed "as they went."

We once again see faith coupled with action when Jesus healed the blind man in the Gospel of John. Christ required the blind man to act before receiving his blessed sight. Christ spit on the ground and made clay that He then applied to the eyes of the blind man. Thereafter, Christ commanded, "'Go, wash in the pool of Siloam' (which is translated, Sent). So he went and washed, and came back seeing" (9:7).

How appropriate that the pool was named *Sent*, for Christ was literally *sending* the blind man to his healing; and in obeying Christ's call to action, the blind man received his sight.

Similarly, the woman with the issue of blood had faith that Jesus could heal her. Matthew 9 says, "She said to herself, 'If only I may touch His garment, I shall be made well'" (v. 21). But it was not until she coupled her faith with her action—namely, pushing through the crowds to grasp the hem of Christ's garment—that her flow of blood immediately ceased.

This woman could have been stoned to death because she was labeled "unclean" and banned from community interaction. And to make matters worse, she had touched a rabbi! Her actions were beyond offensive according to the law. But she was sick and tired of being sick and tired! She had sufficient faith to know that if she could only touch the Master's garment, she would receive her blessing. Christ confirmed her healing by saying, "Be of good cheer, daughter; your faith has made you well" (Matthew 9:22).

Romans 10:17 says that "faith comes by hearing, and hearing by the word of God." Believers build their faith by hearing the promises of God and reading about the great examples of faith found within the Word. Look no further than Hebrews 11 to see a list of the heroes of the faith. From Abraham, Isaac, and Jacob to Noah and Moses, the list goes on and on. But this *who's who* of righteous faith is by no means an exhaustive list. In citing their names, the writer of Hebrews adds: "What more shall I say? For the time would fail me to tell . . . who . . . obtained a good testimony through faith" (vv. 32–39).

I am encouraged to see that this long and prestigious list, by the author's own admission, is incomplete. This lets me know that in the annals of God there is still room for people like you and me to exercise our faith—to put our faith into action and not only receive His blessings but also attain a good testimony through our faith.

The God of the Bible is a God of love, grace, mercy, forgiveness, peace, hope, creative power, and divine order. Everything God has done or will do is completed to perfection: "being confident of this very thing, that He who has begun a good work in you will complete it until the day of Jesus Christ" (Philippians 1:6).

The sun, moon, and stars move with such divine order and precision that the atomic clock that boasts of being accurate within one second every ten years is set by the stars—by God's creation! There is also divine order in the matter of releasing the supernatural power of the Prophetic Blessing.

Numbers 6:27 confirms this, saying, "So they [those in spiritual authority] shall put My name on the children of Israel." The word "*so*" makes it clear that the exact instructions God has just given in the preceding text are to be carried out exactly in order to release His blessing.

SIX SCRIPTURAL REQUIREMENTS FOR RELEASING AND RECEIVING THE PROPHETIC BLESSING

1. The Prophetic Blessing is to be imparted by a person in spiritual authority.

It must be reiterated that the blessing belongs to God. He instructed Aaron and the priests to be His delegated spiritual authority—they were the pipeline through which the Prophetic Blessing flowed.

Speak to Aaron and his sons saying, "This is the way you shall bless the children of Israel." (Numbers 6:23)

Aaron was the high priest of Israel, and his sons were of the tribe of Levi, which constituted the priesthood. They were the spiritual authority of the nation of Israel. Jesus Christ belonged to the tribe of Judah; He was not a Levite. Nonetheless, Christ became our High Priest, as Hebrews 7:14–17 records:

For it is evident that our Lord arose from Judah, of which tribe Moses spoke nothing concerning priesthood. And it is yet far more evident if, in the likeness of Melchizedek, there arises another priest who has come, not according to the law of a fleshly commandment, but according to the power of an endless life. For He testifies:

"You are a priest forever
According to the order of Melchizedek."

The point of logic is that the men of the tribe of Levi in the Old Testament were priests by birth. The priesthood of the believer was passed to Jesus Christ by His death and resurrection on the cross as "a priest forever" (Psalms 110:4; Hebrews 7:17).

When a person becomes a believer in Jesus Christ, he is a "living stone," according to 1 Peter 2:5: "You also, as living stones, are being built up a spiritual house, a holy priesthood, to offer up spiritual sacrifices acceptable to God through Jesus Christ."

Every believer becomes a living stone at the moment of conversion. We are a holy priesthood, and later St. Peter called us a "royal priesthood" (1 Peter 2:9). Therefore, believers—both men and women—have the spiritual authority to release the blessing of God upon their children as well as receive the blessing from their spiritual authority.

2. The Prophetic Blessing shall be given while standing.

In Scripture, *standing* is a sign of reverence and respect. Every priest stood when he ministered to the people. The people stood while Solomon dedicated the Temple. Jesus stands at the right hand of God.

> *At that time the LORD separated the tribe of Levi to bear the ark of the covenant of the LORD, to stand before the LORD to minister to Him and to bless in His name, to this day. (Deuteronomy 10:8)*

> *Then the king turned around and blessed the whole assembly of Israel, while all the assembly of Israel was standing. (2 Chronicles 6:3)*

Yet they shall be ministers in My sanctuary, as gatekeepers of the house and ministers of the house; they shall slay the burnt offering and the sacrifice for the people, and they shall stand before them to minister to them. (Ezekiel 44:11)

Then the Lord said to [Moses], "Take your sandals off your feet, for the place where you stand is holy ground." (Acts 7:33)

But [Stephen], being full of the Holy Spirit, gazed into heaven and saw the glory of God, and Jesus standing at the right hand of God. (Acts 7:55)

In the US military, when an officer walks into the room, everyone of a lower rank stands in unison and salutes. I have had the honor of visiting many of the prime ministers of Israel, and when they walk into a room, everyone immediately stands to give tribute and show honor to the highest office in the land. When I read the scriptural text before I preach to the membership of Cornerstone Church, I call them to stand in honor of the Word of God.

Many reliable scriptural accounts confirm that one must stand when releasing the Prophetic Blessing, in reverence to God, who is ultimately bestowing the blessing upon His children through His Word.

3. When the delegated spiritual authority is speaking the Prophetic Blessing over someone, he or she does so with uplifted hands.

Then Aaron lifted his hand *toward the people, blessed them, and came down from offering the sin offering, the burnt offering, and peace offerings. (Leviticus 9:22)*

And [Jesus] led [the disciples] out as far as Bethany, and He lifted up His hands *and blessed them. (Luke 24:50)*

Raised hands in Judaism are the physical portrait of the blessing, which contains fifteen words. Each of the fifteen words corresponds to a different part of the hand. The palm of the hand represents the last word (*shalom* or *peace*). "The spiritual authority who raises their hands with palms outward while praying alludes to the peace of God without which there can be no blessing."[4]

4. The Prophetic Blessing must be done in the name of the Lord.

So they shall put My name on the children of Israel, and I will bless them. (Numbers 6:27)

Then he may serve in the name of the LORD His God as all his brethren the Levites do, who stand there before the LORD. (Deuteronomy 18:7)

Then the priests, the sons of Levi, shall come near, for the Lord *your God has chosen them to minister to Him and to bless in the* name of the Lord. *(Deuteronomy 21:5)*

And whatever you do in word or deed, do all in the name of the Lord Jesus. *(Colossians 3:17)*

When invoking the blessing, *Kohanim* (Levitical priests) literally place their hands on the forehead of the person receiving the Prophetic Blessing and trace the Hebrew name of the Lord with their fingertips.

God's recipe for spiritual revival in America is found in 2 Chronicles 7:14: "If My people who are called by *My name* will humble themselves, and pray and seek My face, and turn from their wicked ways, then will I hear from heaven, and will forgive their sin and will heal their land."

Second Chronicles 6:6 states, "Yet I have chosen Jerusalem, that *My name* may be there . . ." Aerial photographs have confirmed God's Word, for they have captured a phenomenom—God, the great I AM, chiseled His name as He formed the mountains around Jerusalem.

But [Jesus] answered and said to [the Pharisees,] "I tell you that if these should keep silent, the stones would immediately cry out." (Luke 19:40)

God will place His Name on the forehead of 144,000 Jewish people who will cover the earth, telling the world that Elijah is coming and that the Messiah is soon to appear. "Then I looked, and behold, a Lamb standing on Mount Zion, and with Him one hundred and forty-four thousand, having *His Father's name* written on their foreheads" (Revelation 14:1).

The Name of God will protect the 144,000 from the anti-Semitic demonic legions that are following the antichrist. Satan, the great imitator, will also put *his* mark on the forehead or right hand of all who follow him (Revelation 13:16–17). The bride of Christ is in heaven watching this global clash of two kingdoms (Revelation 4). Where will you be?

5. The Prophetic Blessing is to be bestowed "face-to-face"!

And Jacob called the name of the place Peniel: "For I have seen God face to face, and my life is preserved." (Genesis 32:30)

So the LORD spoke to Moses face to face, as a man speaks to his friend. (Exodus 33:11)

And they will tell it to the inhabitants of this land. They have heard that You, LORD, are among these people; that You, LORD, are seen face to face and Your cloud stands

above them, and You go before them in a pillar of cloud
by day and in a pillar of fire by night. (Numbers 14:14)

The mandate in Numbers 6:23 states, "Say to them," which means "as a person speaks with his friend face to face."[5] God spoke with Jacob and Moses face-to-face. Following His resurrection, Jesus met with His disciples several times face-to-face (Luke 24:36). One who is ready to receive the Prophetic Blessing does so with intent, standing before his or her delegated spiritual authority—face-to-face. When we stand before the Lord in heaven to receive His blessing—"Well done, good and faithful servant"—it will be face-to-face (Matthew 25:23).

6. The Prophetic Blessing is to be given with the voice of authority that all can hear.

And the Levites [priests] shall speak with a loud voice and
say to all the men of Israel. (Deuteronomy 27:14)

Divine proclamations are not mousy! When you pray, angels are listening and demons are trembling. When you give a prophetic proclamation, all present should be able to hear you. In Judaism, if a rabbi is too weak to speak loudly enough for all to hear, he is not allowed to give the blessing.[6] When you speak anything pertaining to the Word of God, be as bold as a lion, and speak without apology to anyone concerning the core values of your faith.

AN OCCASION TO BLESS

Jesus said, "Therefore whoever hears these sayings of Mine, and does them, I will liken him to a wise man who built his house on the rock" (Matthew 7:24). In this verse Jesus made the sharp distinction between *hearing* the Word and *doing* the Word.

While it is inspirational to read or talk about the power of the Prophetic Blessing, it is better to declare it over your spouse, your children, your grandchildren, and your fellow believers, and it is far better to receive the Prophetic Blessing.

Jewish fathers and mothers pray the blessing over their children every Sabbath. The blessing can be given by the mother or the father at any time of the day. Blessing your children each day before they leave for school or before they go to bed is a deed you will never regret and a blessing your children will never forget.

The other morning I quietly walked into my daughter Tina's home and saw her place her hands on the head of her daughter, Micah, before she left for a math competition. I overheard her utter the Prophetic Blessing over her child. An even more beautiful sight was Micah reverently standing in front of her mother, eagerly receiving every word coming from the mouth of her spiritual authority.

Before my daughter and son-in-law, Sandy and Ryan, left on a recent trip, they gathered their two daughters, Olivia and Ellie, to pray a blessing of protection, peace, and joy over them. Sandy recounted that when Ryan was done, five-year-old Olivia began to weep. When they asked her why she was crying, she answered, "Daddy, your prayer made me feel so good. I am crying because I feel happy."

God is the source of every blessing and has chosen to release the Prophetic Blessing over your life through spiritual authority. God is ready and willing to open the windows of heaven and bless you with blessings you cannot possibly contain. "Every good gift [blessing] and every perfect gift is from above, and comes down from the Father of lights, with whom there is no variation or shadow of turning" (James 1:17).

God has done His part; now you must do yours. If your spiritual authority has, by inspiration of the Holy Spirit, proclaimed through the Prophetic Blessing that you will be the best salesman in your company, is it sufficient to receive the blessing and then just lie on the couch waiting for it to manifest? No! You must receive your Prophetic Blessing and take action; prepare yourself and then go out and do your best to accomplish that which has been spoken into your life. Remember this truth: "Faith without works is dead" (James 2:20).

Receiving the Prophetic Blessing requires a conscious decision and action on your part. The Prophetic Blessing will never manifest itself in your life until *you*, in faith, joyously receive and take positive action on what God has divinely ordained.

If it were not for the power of the Word of God that was spoken over my life years ago through His Prophetic Blessing, I would never have known my divine destiny, which is still alive and burning within me today.

Chapter Eleven

PROCLAIMING THE PROPHETIC BLESSING

But you are a chosen generation, a royal priesthood, a holy
nation, His own special people, that you may proclaim the praises
of Him who called you out of darkness into His marvelous light.

—1 PETER 2:9

The phrase *to proclaim* comes from the Latin phrase
meaning "to shout forth." A biblical proclamation is an
official declaration of God's Word over the life of the believer.
Every proclamation should be based upon one or more scriptures that apply to your specific need.

On one occasion when my dear friend Rabbi Scheinberg
and I were discussing the Torah, he passionately described
his love for the Word: "I believe that the Word is God and
God is the Word. I believe that the *Shekinah* [the Holy Spirit]

abides between the Hebrew letters of the written Word, and as the letters leap upward, they are like the cloven tongues of fire giving the Word life! I believe that the Word is dynamic [alive and powerful], which is why the believer can read a Scripture verse one day and it mean one thing and read the same verse another day and it means another!"

❧ THINK ON THIS ❧

You do not read the Word; the Word reads you and brings heaven's answers.

After you have defined your specific circumstance, allow the Holy Spirit to reveal the scriptures that will empower you to receive your blessing. Once you have identified them, begin to proclaim God's promises over your life.

There is a miracle in your mouth activated by the living Word of God. King David wrote, "Hear my prayer, O God; give ear to the words of my mouth" (Psalm 54:2) and "I cried out to him with my mouth; his praise was on my tongue" (Psalm 66:17 NIV).

Proceed from reading the Scripture aloud to systematic memorization of the Word. King David declared, "Your word I have hidden in my heart, that I might not sin against You" (Psalm 119:11). The phrase *hidden in my heart* means to memorize. The Hebrew expression *to learn by heart* is *to learn by mouth*.

Torah-believing Jews begin their morning prayers by putting on their *tallit* (prayer shawl) and strapping their tefillin/phylacteries (small boxes that contain parchment scrolls of Scripture) on their left hand and head as they proclaim the Word of God. The writings placed within these boxes are Exodus 13:1–16 and Deuteronomy 6:4–9, 13–21.

Deuteronomy 6:4–9 proclaims, "Hear, O Israel: The LORD our God, the LORD is one. You shall love the LORD your God with all your heart, with all your soul, and with all your might. And these words which I command you today shall be in your heart; you shall teach them diligently to your children, and shall talk of them when you sit in your house, when you walk by the way, when you lie down, and when you rise up. You shall bind them as a sign on your hand and they shall be as frontlets between your eyes. You shall write them on the doorposts of your house and your gates."

Some Jewish sages believe that "the wearing of tefillin is one commandment that even God observes."[1] Imagine it! Jesus, a rabbi who lived by the law of Moses, put on His prayer shawl and placed the tefillin on His hand and head every morning before prayer as He quoted the prophet Hosea: "I will betroth you to Me forever; yes, I will betroth you to Me in righteousness and justice, in lovingkindness and mercy; I will betroth you to Me in faithfulness, and you shall know the LORD" (2:19–20).

If the Son of God considered proclaiming the Word crucial to His daily ministry, how much more should we?

I WILL RESCUE

I am the LORD; I will bring you out from under the bur-
dens of the Egyptians. I will rescue you from their bond-
age . . . and I will redeem you with an outstretched arm.
(Exodus 6:6)

In 2008, I was admitted to the hospital for quadruple-by-
pass surgery. On the day of my surgery, the hospital gra-
ciously made a large room available for people who came
from all over America to prayerfully read the Word of God
aloud during my six-hour surgery. I am a firm believer that
when the Word of God is read audibly, the powers and principalities of darkness are bound and defeated.

As the surgical team rolled the gurney into my room, I
was proclaiming Psalm 91. I was saturating my mind, body,
and spirit with the Word of God, declaring the final three
verses of this psalm:

"Because he loves me," says the LORD, "I will rescue him;
I will protect him, for he acknowledges my name.
He will call upon me, and I will answer him;
I will be with him in trouble,
I will deliver him and honor him.
With long life will I satisfy him
and show him my salvation." (vv. 14–16 NIV)

I climbed up on the gurney and kissed Diana and my children before they rolled me to surgery.

I remember telling Diana, "I don't want you to host a party in there . . . I want prayer!" Diana promised that they would cover me in prayer the whole time I was in surgery. She immediately went into the room where the people were gathered and sat down at the head of the table where she was surrounded by about twenty prayer warriors. Diana began by reading Psalm 1: "Blessed is the man . . ." As she finished, the next person began reading the next psalm. Though the minutes ticked by slowly, my prayer warriors never let a moment lapse without proclaiming the Word. Psalm after psalm, every verse was read.

After I had been in surgery several hours, Rabbi Scheinberg joined the group and randomly took his place in the circle. When it was his turn to proclaim the Word, the next psalm to be read was—are you ready?—Psalm 91! He began at verse one, and while he was reading the last three verses (vv. 14–16), the surgeon called to say that the surgery was over and that I was doing very well.

There is no happenstance in the life of the believer. God's timing is always perfect. He allowed the exact chapter and verse to be read in my *"going out and coming in"* (Psalm 121:8) as a sign from heaven that He was in total control of my life. It was God's assurance to me and to my loved ones that He wasn't finished with me yet. I thank God for the power of the Prophetic Blessing every day of my life!

Now it is your opportunity to receive and proclaim what God has ordained for you.

PROCLAMATIONS

It is my desire to equip you in declaring God's Word over your life and the lives of your loved ones. Speak the Word of God over your children and grandchildren, over your spouse, over your business; declare His promises over someone who is sick and needs divine healing, someone who is going through a great personal trial, someone in desperate need of emotional stability, someone who wants to attack their lack and discover God's prosperity—someone who desires the favor of God.

I offer you the following proclamations that will help you begin your exciting journey of worry-free living. God wants you to have peace that surpasses understanding, joy that is unspeakable, and love that is boundless, rich, and pure—He wants you to live the good life!

Proclamation over Your Children and Grandchildren

Heavenly Father, God of Abraham, Isaac, and Jacob, I place my hands on the head of my child _____ as Jesus did in His earthly ministry.

May he/she know You early in his/her life. May he/she learn to hear Your voice and obey Your commandments.

I ask You, Lord God, to bless my son/daughter in his/

her going out and coming in. May You send Your angels before my son/daughter to prepare his/her way, to protect him/her from all harm and danger, to be his/her rear guard.

Bring him/her godly friends and prepare the spouse intended for him/her who will love my son/daughter second only to You.

Bring to _____ the blessings of Abraham to be his/her portion. May he/she prosper and do well; may everything he/she touches be blessed of God.

Bless his/her heart, soul, mind, and body to be consecrated to the purposes of God. May the grace and peace of God rest upon _____ now and forever. In Jesus' name, Amen!

Proclamation over Your Wife

Heavenly Father, God of Abraham, Isaac, and Jacob, as the priest of my house, I place my hands on the head of my wife _____ and proclaim this blessing.

Let her life be as the life of Ruth—blessed and highly favored in all things. Give to her the desires of her heart, and richly bless everything she puts her hand to.

She is worth more than rubies; her presence brings the light of God into our home. _____ is clothed with strength and honor, she speaks with wisdom, and the law of love rules the speech of her mouth. Give to my wife _____ the reward she has earned and let her works praise her in the mouths of our family and friends. In Jesus' name, I speak and release this blessing over my precious wife _____. Amen!

Proclamation over Your Business

Heavenly Father, God of Abraham, Isaac, and Jacob, I proclaim today that this business is Your business, for every good and perfect gift comes from God our Father above. I ask You, as did Jabez: "Oh, that You would bless me indeed, and enlarge my territory, that Your hand would be with me, and that You would keep me from evil, that I may not cause pain" (1 Chronicles 4:10)!

I confess with my mouth that it is the Lord who gives me power to get wealth. It is the Lord who opens the windows of heaven to send blessings to me that are above and beyond what I can ask or imagine. It is the Lord who delights in the prosperity of the righteous.

Therefore, Lord God, open the windows of heaven and bless our business that Your name might be glorified and all my needs shall be met. In Jesus' name, Amen!

Proclamation for Health and Healing

Heavenly Father, God of Abraham, Isaac, and Jacob, I place the anointing oil (James 5:14) on the head of _____ believing that You are the God who heals all our sicknesses and infirmities.

May the hands of earthly physicians be led by the hands of the Great Physician. [To be used for someone in the hospital awaiting surgery.]

Lord, in Your earthly ministry You were a miraculous healer. The Word of God declares that Jesus Christ is the same yesterday, today, and forever. What You did on the shores of Galilee You can do today.

Your Word declares, "But those who wait on the LORD shall renew their strength; they shall mount up with wings like eagles, they shall run and not be weary, they shall walk and not faint" (Isaiah 40:31).

Your Word declares from the mouth of King David, "He sent His word and healed them" (Psalm 107:20).

Lord God, in the authority of Your name, we receive health and healing today for _____. In Jesus' name, Amen!

Proclamation in a Time of Testing and Trial

Heavenly Father, God of Abraham, Isaac, and Jacob, we come before You today on behalf of _____ who is going through a time of testing and trial.

We proclaim the words of St. Paul, who said, "But thanks be to God, who gives us the victory through our Lord Jesus Christ. Therefore, my beloved brethren, be steadfast, immovable, always abounding in the work of the Lord, knowing that your labor is not in vain in the Lord" (1 Corinthians 15:57–58).

We proclaim the words of St. Peter: "Blessed be the God and Father of our Lord Jesus Christ, who according to His abundant mercy has begotten us again to a living hope through the resurrection of Jesus Christ from the dead. . . . In this you greatly rejoice, though now for a little while, if need be, you have been grieved by various trials, that the genuineness of your faith, being much more precious than gold . . . though it is tested by fire, may be found to praise, honor, and glory at the revelation of Jesus Christ, whom having not seen you love" (1 Peter 1:3, 6–8). We receive grace and peace for _____ knowing that the mercies of God endure forever. Amen.

Proclamation for Emotional Stability

Heavenly Father, God of Abraham, Isaac, and Jacob, we come before You today on behalf of _____ that You would grant to our servant grace and peace.

Jesus said, and we proclaim, "Come to Me, all you who labor and are heavy laden, and I will give you rest. Take My yoke upon you and learn from Me, for I am gentle and lowly in heart, and you will find rest for your souls. For My yoke is easy and My burden is light" (Matthew 11:28–30).

We proclaim, "My peace I give to you; not as the world gives do I give to you. Let not your heart be troubled, neither let it be afraid" (John 14:27).

"You will keep him in perfect peace whose mind is stayed on You, because he trusts in You" (Isaiah 26:3).

"God has not given us a spirit of fear, but of power and of love and of a sound mind" (2 Timothy 1:7).

"Now may the God of hope fill you with all joy and peace in believing, that you may abound in hope by the power of the Holy Spirit" (Romans 15:13).

"And the peace of God, which surpasses all understanding, will guard your hearts and minds through Christ Jesus. Finally, brethren, whatever things are true, whatever things are noble, whatever things are just, whatever things are pure, whatever things are lovely, whatever things are of good report . . . meditate on these things" (Philippians 4:7–8).

Therefore, may the peace of God that surpasses all understanding be _____ portion in Jesus' mighty Name! Amen.

Proclamation for the Favor of God

Heavenly Father, God of Abraham, Isaac, and Jacob, I come before You today as Your child seeking Your divine favor.

Lord God, Your favor surrounds the righteous. In faith believing, I receive the favor of God now in every dimension of my life. Let the favor of God rest upon every member of my family. Let Your favor rest upon our health, our finances, and our relationships.

Lord God, from this day forward I am going to receive the limitless favor of God—supernatural increase, promotion, restoration, honor, spiritual victories, petitions granted, and battles won that I don't have to fight. The favor of God is upon me; it goes before me, and therefore, my life will never be the same. In Jesus' name, Amen!

Proclamation for Divine Prosperity

Heavenly Father, God of Abraham, Isaac, and Jacob, I come to You today as Your servant who believes in, trusts in, and relies on the Lord, and whose hope and confidence is in the Lord (Jeremiah 17:7).

I proclaim today the words of King David: "Delight yourself also in the Lord, and He shall give you the desires of your heart" (Psalm 37:4).

"No good thing will [the Lord] withhold from those who walk uprightly" (Psalm 84:11).

"And my God shall supply all your need according to His riches in glory by Christ Jesus" (Philippians 4:19).

I proclaim the Word of the Lord: "Beloved, I pray that you may prosper in all things and be in health, just as your soul prospers" (3 John 2).

Today, I delight myself in You, Lord, who gives me the desires and secret petitions of my heart. As my heavenly Father, You know what I need before I ask and generously supply my every need according to Your riches in glory in Christ Jesus. As I devote my heart and soul to seeking You, I will prosper in every way, even as my soul prospers.

When I honor You, Father God, with a tenth of my income and that tithe is given as firstfruits, You will open the floodgates of heaven and pour out abundant blessings. I thank You, Father, for Your blessings and favor, knowing every good and perfect gift comes from You. Amen!

It is time to release the power of the Prophetic Blessing. Prepare yourself by seeking the Lord in prayer. Then stand, extend your hands toward your loved one, and repeat the Priestly Blessing over him or her. Now continue by proclaiming aloud the Holy Spirit-directed Prophetic Blessing over your loved one's life.

"AND MAY THE LORD BLESS YOU AND KEEP YOU . . ."

The power and majesty of the Prophetic Blessings of God to His people have been unveiled to you. God blessed Abraham, Isaac, Jacob, and Jacob's twelve sons, who served Him with their hearts and lives in the Old Testament through the fulfillment of the Prophetic Blessing they received.

Jesus Christ blessed His followers in the New Testament with eight Prophetic Blessings imparted on a mountainside in Galilee, which transformed their lives and created the blueprint for the future of Christianity. Now God desires to bless you as you commit your heart and life in full surrender to do His will.

You have discovered the *ruach* first seen in the book of Genesis as God revealed it through creation, through the prophets, and then through the Prophetic Blessings chronicled in the life and ministry of Jesus Christ.

When you proclaim God's Word to your family, it transforms your life and the lives of your family members. You have been liberated to receive the Prophetic Blessing over your personal life.

But what about the man or woman who has never been blessed by their spiritual authority? Perhaps your parents have gone to glory before discovering the Prophetic Blessing. Perhaps your parents have no relationship with the Lord. Perhaps your pastor does not teach or believe in the power of the Prophetic Blessing. What now? Can you still receive the Prophetic Blessing? The answer is a resounding YES!

Think of Jacob who wrestled with God—he passionately desired God's blessing: "But [Jacob] said, 'I will not let You go unless You bless me!'" (Genesis 32:26).

Jacob, "the heel catcher," would not let God go until he was blessed and transformed into his divine destiny as "Israel": "And [God] said, 'Your name shall no longer be called Jacob, but Israel; for you have struggled with God and with men, and have prevailed'" (v. 28).

Had Jacob not wrestled with God and insisted on receiving his blessing, his name would not have been changed to Israel and his destiny would have been denied. It is in the *wrestling* that the transformation occurs.

You too can prevail over your struggles by receiving the Prophetic Blessing from the throne of God, for He has "called you out of darkness and into His marvelous light" (1 Peter 2:9).

I close this book with the following blessing, which will enable you to hear what God your Father and Jesus your High Priest desire for your life through the Word. I am asking you to receive this Prophetic Blessing in faith, believing! This one act of obedience can change the course of your life as you begin your journey toward your divine destiny:

Heavenly Father, in the Name of Jesus Christ our High Priest, I come before Your throne today, and I speak this blessing: May the Lord bless you and keep you; and may the Lord make His face to shine upon you; may the Lord be gracious unto you and lift up His countenance upon you; and may the Lord give you His peace.

Lord God, I ask You in the Name above every name that You open the windows of heaven and pour out divine provision upon every one of Your children.

Heavenly Father, in this time of economic crisis, let those who hear this blessing receive the best of things in the worst of times from Jehovah Jireh, the Lord our Provider. I speak and release health and healing to every physical body. I come against every form of infirmity; I come against every form of sickness and disease; I come against every physical malady in the name of Jesus Christ, and

I declare that these sicknesses and diseases are cursed at the root and that the blessing of divine health freely flows into their lives like streams of living water.

Lord, I speak peace to every life that is in torment, for Your name is Jehovah Shalom, the Lord our Peace. I give You praise, Father, that the enemy has been defeated and the peace of God that surpasses all understanding has now healed every broken heart. Every sorrow is being lifted right now; every burden and yoke is being destroyed by Your mighty right hand. O Lord our God, You are our Joy in the morning.

You, O Lord, are our Strength, our High Tower, our Shield and our Buckler, a shelter in the time of storm. You are our Song; You are our Righteousness; You are our Shepherd, our Great Physician, and the Giver of life. We magnify Your Holy Name.

Let the power of this Prophetic Blessing rest upon you and in you, and may it be imparted by you as you proclaim the Word of God in the authority of Jesus' Name.

So they shall put My name of the children of Israel and I will bless them. (Numbers 6:27)

NOTES

CHAPTER 1: THE POWER OF THE PROPHETIC BLESSING

1. Dan Senor and Saul Singer, *Startup Nation: The Story of Israel's Economic Miracle* (New York: Twelve/Hachette Book Group, 2009), 13-15.
2. David Brooks, "The Tel Aviv Cluster," *New York Times*, January 11, 2010; http://www.nytimes.com/2010/01/12/opinion/12brooks .html.

CHAPTER 2: BORN TO BE BLESSED

1. Tim Hegg, "The Priestly Blessing," Nisan 4, 5761, *Bikurie Zion* 2001; http://www.torahresource.com/EnglishArticles/Aaronic%20 Ben.pdf. All rights reserved.
2. Rabbi Avie Gold, ArtScroll Mesorah Series, *Bircas Kohanim* (Brooklyn, NY: Mesorah Publications, July 1986), 763.
3. Hegg, *The Priestly Blessing*.
4. Ibid.
5. Ibid.
6. Ibid.
7. Ibid.
8. Gold, *Bircas Kohanim*, 765.
9. Hegg, *The Priestly Blessing*.
10. Larry Finn, "The Blessing of the Jewish Priest," *The Jewish Magazine*, August 2007; http://www.jewishmag.com/116mag/ cohen/cohen.htm.
11. Ibid.
12. Hegg, "The Priestly Blessing."
13. Adapted from Tim Hegg, "The Priestly Blessing."

CHAPTER 3: THE GENESIS BLESSING

1. Rabbi Meir Zlotowitz, *Bereishis*, Genesis Section 1, ArtScroll Series, (Brooklyn, NY: Mesorah Publications, 1988), 2.
2. Oral Roberts, *The Fourth Man and Other Famous Sermons* (Tulsa, OK: Healing Waters, Inc., 1953), 20.
3. *Matthew Henry's Commentary on the Whole Bible* (Peabody, MA: Hendrickson Publishing), 16.
4. Rabbi Meir Zlotowitz and Rabbi Nosson Scherman, gen. eds., *The Chumash*, The Stone Edition, ArtScroll Series (Brooklyn, NY: Mesorah Publications, January 2001), 73.
5. "Abortion Statistics," *National Right to Life* (1973–2010); http://www.nrlc.org/factsheets/fs03_abortionintheus.pdf.
6. *Prophecy Study Bible*, John C. Hagee, gen. ed. (Nashville, TN: Thomas Nelson Publishers, 1997), 7.

CHAPTER 4: THE ABRAHAMIC BLESSING

1. "Israel, A Nation of Miracles," *The Herald of Christ's Kingdom*; http://www.heraldmag.org/olb/contents/doctrine/israel%20a%20nation%20of%20miracles.htm.
2. Ibid.
3. Ibid.
4. Ibid.
5. Ibid.
6. Ibid.

CHAPTER 5: TO BLESS OR NOT TO BLESS?

1. These books I've authored include: *The Beginning of the End* (Nashville, TN: Thomas Nelson, 1996); *Battle for Jerusalem* (Nashville, TN: Thomas Nelson, 2003); *Jerusalem Countdown* (Lake Mary, FL: Frontline, 2006); *In Defense of Israel* (Lake Mary, FL: Frontline, 2007).
2. Adapted from various teachings by Pastor John Hagee included in *In Defense of Israel*.

3. "At Least Killed on Gaza Flotilla," *Daily Alert,* May 31, 2010; http://youtu.be/Q8pDfH7b0Gs.

4. Ibid.

5. "Righteous Among the Nations," *Encyclopedia Judaica;* also available online at *Jewish Virtual Library:* http://www.jewish virtuallibrary.org/jsource/judaica/ejud_0002_0017_0_16756.html.

6. Ibid.

7. *The Oskar Schindler Story*; www.oskarschindler.com.

8. "Righteous Among the Nations," *Encyclopedia Judaica.*

9. Ibid.

10. Corrie ten Boom, *The Hiding Place* (Grand Rapids, MI: Chosen Books, 1976, 2006).

11. Righteous Among the Nations," *Encyclopedia Judaica.*

12. Ibid.

13. Ibid.

14. Ibid.

15. Ibid.

16. Ibid.

17. Hagee, *In Defense of Israel.*

18. Ibid.

19. Lt. Col. (ret.) Jonathan D. Halevi, "Al-Queda: The Next Goal Is to Liberate Spain from the Infidels," Jerusalem Center for Public Affairs, vol.7, no.16, October 11, 2007.

20. Derek Prince, *Promised Land* (Grand Rapids, MI: Baker Books, 2005), 43.

21. John Hagee, AIPAC National Policy Conference, March 11, 2007.

22. Michael Birnbaum, "European Debt Crisis: Greek Bailout Talks are Complicated by Looming Deadline," *The Washington Post*, February 15, 2012.

23. Halevi, "Al-Queda: The Next Goal Is to Liberate Spain from the Infidels."

24. Heather Horn, "Germany's New Old Problem: The Rise of Neo-Nazi Violence," *The Atlantic*, November 15, 2007.

25. Steven L. Pease, *The Golden Age of Jewish Achievement* (Queensland, Australia: Deucalion, 2009), 238.

26. Israel Peri-Urban Agriculture; www.cityfarmer.org/israel periurban.html.

27. Pease, *The Golden Age of Jewish Achievement*, ix.

28. Nadav Shemer, "Israeli Cows Outperform Their Foreign Counterparts," *The Jerusalem*, June 7, 2011.

29. Haaretz, "Fewer Farmers—More Produce," www.Haaretz.com/ themarker/business-in-brief-1.318542.

30. Derek Prince, *Our Debt to Israel* (Derek Prince Ministries-International, 1984), 7.

31. Adapted from actual events chronicled in Hagee, *In Defense of Israel*.

CHAPTER 6: THE BLESSINGS FULFILLED

1. John Phillips, *Exploring Genesis: An Expository Commentary* (Grand Rapids, MI: Kregel Publications, 1980), 362.

2. Ibid., 362-364.

3. Ibid.

4. Arthur A. Pink, *Gleanings in Genesis* (Chicago: Moody Press, 1922), 324.

5. J. Vernon McGee, *Thru the Bible*, Volume 1: Genesis through Deuteronomy (Nashville, TN: Thomas Nelson Publishers, 1981), 193-194.

6. Pink, *Gleanings in Genesis*, 327.

7. Ibid., 328.

8. Ibid., 330-331.

9. Ibid.

10. Ibid., 335.

11. Ethan Bronner, "Gas Field Confirmed Off Coast of Israel," *The New York Times*, December 30, 2010; http://www.nytimes .com/2010/12/31/world/middleeast/31leviathan.html.

12. Phillips, *Exploring Genesis*, 370.

13. John Hagee, *In Defense of Israel* (Lake Mary, FL: Frontline, 2007), 222-226.

14. Rabbi Nosson Scherman and Rabbi Meir Ziotowitz, gen. eds., *The Chumash*, The Stone Edition, ArtScroll Series (Brooklyn, NY: Mesorah Publications, 1993), 283.

15. Derek Prince, *The Divine Exchange* (Derek Prince Ministries-International, 1955), 5.

CHAPTER 7: THE EIGHT PROPHETIC BLESSINGS OF JESUS

1. Patsy Clairmont, *God Uses Cracked Pots* (Colorado Springs, CO: Focus on the Family, 1991).

2. "Record percentage of U.S. children born out of wedlock," *EWTN News,* April 11, 2010; http://www.ewtnnews.com/catholic-news/US.php?id = 358.

3. "Consequences of father absence," *Fathers For Life*; http://fathersforlife.org/divorce/chldrndiv.htm.

4. "Statistics on Teenage Drug Use," *Teen Drug Abuse;* http://www.teendrugabuse.us/teen_drug_use.html.

5. National School Safety Center report (includes school-associated violent deaths on private or public school property for kindergarten through grade 12). http://www.schoolsafety.us/media-resources/school-associated-violent-deaths.

6. John Thomas Didymus, "Wicca is America's fastest growing religion, says Witch School"; http://digitaljournal.com/article/313379.

7. "Pagan stone circle built at US Air Force training academy," *The Telegraph,* November 28, 2011; http://www.telegraph.co.uk/news/newstopics/howaboutthat/8920124/Pagan-stone-circle-built-at-US-Air-Force-training-academy.html.

8. Matt Clarke, "Celebrity Justice: Prison Lifestyles of the Rich and Famous," *Prison Legal News*; https://www.prisonlegalnews.org/(S(myhtoimek3qnv445vssf5xb0))/displayArticle.aspx?articleid = 22532&AspxAutoDetectCookieSupport = 1.

9. Adam Nagourney, "Court Strikes Down Ban on Gay Marriage in California," *New York Times*, February 7, 2012; http://www.nytimes.com/2012/02/08/us/marriage-ban-violates-constitution-court-rules.html.

10. Theodore Roosevelt, "The Strenuous Life," speech before the Hamilton Club, Chicago, IL, April 10, 1899; http://www.bartleby.com/58/1.html.

11. Winston Churchill, "Blood, Toil, Tears, and Sweat," speech before the House of Commons, London, May 13, 1940; http://www.winstonchurchill.org/learn/speeches-of-winston-churchill/1940-finest-hour/92-blood-toil-tears-and-sweat.

CHAPTER 8: RELEASING THE PROPHETIC BLESSING THROUGH THE SPOKEN WORD

1. Oscar Hammerstein, "A Bell Is No Bell," lyrics from *The Sound of Music*, in *The Complete Lyrics of Oscar Hammerstein II*, ed. Amy Asch (New York: Knopf, 2008), 396.

2. "The Power of Speech," Judaism 101, www.jewfaq.org/speech.htm.

3. Cardinal Richelieu, *Testament Politique*, http://quotes.yourdictionary.com/sword.

4. Robyn Freedman Spizman, *Chief Joseph, When Words Matter Most* (New York: Crown Publishers, 1996), 67.

5. E. C. McKenzie, *Mac's Giant Book of Quips and Quotes* (Eugene, OR: Harvest House Publishers, 1980), 562.

6. Ibid.

7. John Phillips, *Exploring Genesis: An Expository Commentary* (Grand Rapids, MI: Kregel Publishers, 2001), 40.

8. Ibid.

9. Wilbur M. Smith, *Therefore Stand* (Grand Rapids, MI: Baker Book House, 1976), as cited by John Phillips in *Exploring Genesis,* 42.

10. Ibid., 43.

11. Derek Prince, *The Power of Proclamation* (Charlotte, NC: Derek Prince Ministries-International, 2002), 11.

12. Ibid., 14.

13. Ibid., 11.

14. Reverend William Bythel Hagee, Dedication Prayer over Pastor John Hagee, October 4, 1987.

15. Adapted from a personal story written in John and Diana Hagee, *What Every Man Wants in a Woman; What Every Woman Wants in a Man* (Lake Mary, FL: Charisma House, 2005), 50–51.

CHAPTER 9: RELEASING THE PROPHETIC BLESSING THROUGH TOUCH

1. "He Touched Me," words and music by Bill Gaither, copyright © 1964 by William J. Gaither. All rights reserved.

2. Tiffany Field, *Touch* (Cambridge, MA: MIT Press, 2003), 17.

3. Mic Hunter and Jim Struve, *The Ethical Use of Touch in Psychotherapy* (Thousand Oaks, CA: Sage Publications, 1998), 13.

4. Ibid.

5. Ibid., 14.

6. Ibid.

7. Ibid.

8. Ibid.

9. Gary Smalley and John Trent, *The Gift of the Blessing* (Nashville, TN: Thomas Nelson, 1993), 45.

10. Ibid.

11. John D. Garr, *Blessings for Family and Friends* (Atlanta, GA: Golden Key Press, 2009), 30.

12. Field, *Touch*, 29.

13. Ibid., 30.

14. Garr, *Blessings for Family and Friends,* 14.

15. Thayer and Smith, *The New Testament Greek Lexicon,* "Ektrepho," public domain.

16. Field, *Touch*, 62.

17. Ibid., 63.

18. Ibid.

19. Ibid.

20. Ibid., 60.

21. Kathleen Keating, *The Hug Therapy Book* (Minneapolis, MN: CompCare Publications, 1983), 340–341.

CHAPTER 10: RECEIVING THE PROPHETIC BLESSING

1. Lillian B. Yeomans, *His Healing Power: Four Classic Books on Healing Complete in One Volume* (Tulsa, OK: Harrison House, 2003), 157.
2. Ibid., 157–158.
3. Ibid., 161.
4. Tim Hegg, "The Priestly Blessing," Nisan 4, 5761, *Bikurie Zion* 2001; http://www.torahresource.com/EnglishArticles/Aaronic%20 Ben.pdf. All rights reserved.
5. Ibid.
6. Ibid.

CHAPTER 11: PROCLAIMING THE PROPHETIC BLESSING

1. George Robinson, *Essential Judaism* (New York: Pocket Books, 2000), 26.

John Hagee is the author of four *New York Times* best-sellers, in addition to *Jerusalem Countdown*, which sold over one million copies. He is the founder and senior pastor of Cornerstone Church in San Antonio, Texas, a non-denominational evangelical church with more than 20,000 active members, as well as the founder and president of John Hagee Ministries, which telecasts his radio and television teachings throughout America and in 249 nations worldwide. Hagee is also the founder and national chairman of Christians United for Israel, a national grassroots association with over one million members to date.

WORTHY
PUBLISHING

IF YOU LIKED THIS BOOK . . .

- Tell your friends by going to: www.thepowerofthe propheticblessing.com and clicking "LIKE"

- Share the video book trailer by posting it on your Facebook page

- Log on to facebook.com/PastorJohnHagee page, click "LIKE" and post a comment regarding what you enjoyed about the book

- Tweet "I recommend reading #poweroftheprophetic blessing by @PastorJohnHagee @Worthypub"

- Hashtag: #Iwasborntobeblessed

- Subscribe to our newsletter by going to www.worthy publishing.com

WORTHY PUBLISHING
FACEBOOK PAGE

WORTHY PUBLISHING
WEBSITE